W9-BEM-912

Chapter 1 Phonics

Table of Contents, continued

Chapter 2 Word Structure

SPECTRUM®

Word Study and Phonics

Grade 3

Spectrum®
An imprint of Carson-Dellosa Publishing LLC
Greensboro, North Carolina

Spectrum®
An imprint of Carson-Dellosa Publishing LLC
P.O. Box 35665
Greensboro, NC 27425 USA

Printed in the USA • All rights reserved.   ISBN 978-1-4838-1184-0

05-080177811

Table of Contents, continued

Lesson 1.1 Beginning Consonants

Look at the pictures below. On the line, write the first letter of the word that names each picture.

____iger   ____eaf   ____ike

____indow   ____urse   ____ear

Read the clues below. Circle the word that matches each clue.

1. I blow air to keep people cool in the summer. What am I?

    can   fan   pan

2. I am fun to read. I can tell a great story. What am I?

    book   hook   look

3. I live in oceans and lakes. Some people keep me as a pet. What am I?

    dish   fish   wish

4. I am a sweet birthday treat. Don't forget to blow out my candles! What am I?

    rake   bake   cake

5. You will find me at the beach. I can be hot to walk on. What am I?

    sand   hand   band

6. I come to your house every day. Sometimes, I travel a long way. What am I?

    mail   rail   sail

Lesson 1.1 Beginning Consonants

Look at the pictures below. Circle the letter that stands for the first sound you hear in each picture name.

m   n   b   b   d   t   s   v   z

p   l   h   v   w   r   f   b   h

Read each sentence below. Then, read the pair of words that follow. On the line, write the word that best completes each sentence.

1. Sam's family has three _____. (dogs, logs)

2. It is Sam's job to _____ them after school.   (talk, walk)

3. Sometimes, he takes them to the _____.   (park, dark)

4. They _____ to swim in the pond and bark at the squirrels.   (dove, love)

5. When Sam whistles, his dogs know it is _____ to go home.   (time, dime)

6. When they are _____, Sam gives each one a treat. (wood, good)

Lesson 1.2 Ending Consonants

Look at the pictures below. On the line, write the last letter of the word that names each picture.

Read each word below. Change the last letter of the word to make a new word. Write the new word on the line. It should rhyme with the three words below it.

1. car _____
        pat   flat   sat

5. sat _____
        tag   bag   flag

2. skim _____
        trip   rip   sip

6. shot _____
        hop   drop   cop

3. bus _____
        rug   shrug   tug

7. hit _____
        slid   rid   lid

4. web _____
        forget set   jet

8. cob _____
        rot   hot   trot

Lesson 1.2 Ending Consonants

When a word ends in a double letter, say the letter's sound only once.

Read the sentences below. Some words are not complete. Add **ss**, **ll**, **ff**, or **zz** to form the word or words that best complete each sentence.

1. The Rileys' goats eat the gra_____ in their yard.

2. Mr. Riley calls them the "Three Billy Goats Gru_____."

3. Maggy Riley brought in one of the goats for show-and-te_____.

4. Her teacher thought the goat might sme_____ or make a me_____.

5. "He might sni_____ our stu_____," said Maggy. "But he won't make a

    me_____."

6. The goat tried to eat a piece of fu_____, a do_____, and a bow on a

    girl's dre_____.

7. "No more animals in cla_____," Maggy's teacher said.

Read each set of words. Circle the word that names each picture.

rat
rag
ran
rap

cut
cup
cub
cuff

pin
pill
pig
pit

Lesson 1.3 Hard and Soft c and g

The letter **c** can make a hard sound, as in *car* and *across*. When **c** is followed by **e**, **i**, or **y**, it can make a soft sound, as in *city* and *fancy*.

The letter **g** can also make a hard sound, as in *gas* and *ago*. When **g** is followed by **e**, **i**, or **y**, it can make a soft sound, as in *gentle* and *age*.

Read the pairs of words below. Write **HC** on the line if they have a hard **c** sound. Write **SC** if they have a soft **c** sound.

1. _____   contest   cabin
2. _____   rice   pencil
3. _____   dancing   cent
4. _____   second   creek
5. _____   price   center
6. _____   crab   cute

Read the pairs of words below. Write **HG** on the line if they have a hard **g** sound. Write **SG** if they have a soft **g** sound.

1. _____   giraffe   orange
2. _____   goldfish garden
3. _____   gem   village
4. _____   signal   frog
5. _____   gate   dragon
6. _____   germ   judge

Lesson 1.3 Hard and Soft c and g

Read the grocery list below. Circle the words that have a hard **c** or **g** sound. Underline the words that have a soft **c** or **g** sound.

Grocery List

grapes	celery	flour
cereal	clams	ice cream
carrots	oranges	sugar
gingerbread	milk	sliced bread
apples	lettuce	eggs
turkey	peanut butter	cat food

Look at each pair of pictures. Draw a line to match the hard or soft sound to each picture.

1. soft **g**   hard **g**

2. hard **c**   soft **c**

3. hard **c**   soft **g**

4. soft **c**   hard **g**

Lesson 1.3 Hard and Soft **c** and **g**

Read the paragraphs below. Look for words with the hard and soft **c** and **g** sounds. Then, write the words in the correct columns. You do not need to list the same word more than once. Hint: One word has both a hard and a soft **c** sound. List it in both columns.

Do you know anyone who collects marbles? Marbles are usually made of clay, glass, or plastic. Most marbles are about the size of a grape. There are a few huge marbles in museums. These giant marbles are about 12 feet tall!

People in many countries play games with marbles. In one game, the players draw a circle in the sand and place their marbles in the circle. They take turns using their marbles to push the other players' marbles out of the circle.

Some marbles are worth a lot of money. The price of a marble has to do with its color, age, and size. If you want to become a collector, join a club or read books to learn which ones are most valuable.

Hard **c**	Soft **c**	Hard **g**	Soft **g**
_____	_____	_____	_____
_____	_____	_____	_____
_____	_____	_____	_____
_____			
_____			
_____			

Lesson 1.3 Hard and Soft c and g

Read the clues below. On the line, write the word that matches each clue. Make sure that the word has the correct hard or soft c or g sound.

1. I live near ponds or creeks. I am green. I make a noise that sounds like *ribbit*. (hard g) _____

2. I come between first and third. I start with the letter s. (hard c) _____

3. I am a tool that is used for writing or drawing. I can be erased. I come in many colors. (soft c) _____

4. People use me when they bake sweet things. I can be brown or white. Some people sprinkle me on cereal or oatmeal. (hard g) _____

5. I am very cold. You can find me in the freezer. I am usually a cube. (soft c) _____

6. I live on a farm. I make milk. I make the sound *moo*. (hard c) _____

7. I am a bright color. I am also the name of a juicy fruit. I am the color of pumpkins. (soft g) _____

8. I come in a box. Lots of people eat me for breakfast. Usually, I am crunchy. (soft c) _____

Review Beginning and Ending Consonants

Look at each picture below. Say its name to yourself. Then, write the missing letter on the line.

ha_____   _____anana   _____angaroo

gra_____   _____ool   she_____

Read each sentence below. Then, read the word beside it. Replace the bold letter to form a word that makes sense in the sentence. Write it on the line.

1. The puffin is a bird that lives _____ the sea. (**f**ear)

2. It has black and white feathers, but its _____ and legs are orange. (bea**d**)

3. The puffin uses its strong _____ to help it swim underwater. (**r**ings)

4. Puffins can _____ several fish in their bills at one time. (**c**old)

5. These seabirds _____ live to be about 25 years old. (ca**p**)

6. Puffins can fly very _____ —about 50 miles per hour. (**l**ast)

7. Some people think puffins _____ a little like penguins. (**b**ook)

Review Hard and Soft **c** and **g**

Say each word to yourself. If it has a hard sound (like *car* or *gas*), circle *hard*. If it has a soft sound, like *city* or *gentle*, circle *soft*.

1. **garden**	hard	soft		5. **danger**	hard	soft
2. **gym**	hard	soft		6. **slice**	hard	soft
3. **attic**	hard	soft		7. **egg**	hard	soft
4. **case**	hard	soft		8. **edge**	hard	soft

Read each bold word below. Decide whether it has a hard or soft sound. Then, circle the word beside it that has the same sound.

1. **guppy**	gem	goat	age
2. **contest**	price	cuddle	decide
3. **cent**	ceiling	card	carrot
4. **guitar**	judge	geese	change
5. **general**	give	began	edge
6. **across**	coat	cent	prince
7. **dragon**	huge	gust	Georgia
8. **face**	traffic	cider	cry
9. **giant**	dog	gown	gel
10. **claw**	crisp	mice	bounce

Lesson 1.4 Beginning Two-Letter Blends with s

Some words begin with two consonants. When the sounds of the consonants are blended together, the two letters are called a **blend**.

Some blends are made with **s** plus another consonant. Each of the words below has an **s** blend.

scare   **sk**ate   **sm**ooth   **sn**icker   **sp**ell   **st**amp   **sw**eat

Say each picture name to yourself. Write the name of the picture on the line. Then, circle the **s** blend.

Read the sentences below. On each line, write an **s** blend from the pair in parentheses ( ). The word you form should make sense in the sentence.

1. Saturday afternoon was cold and _____owy. (sp, sn)

2. Carson and Samir decided to go _____ating on the frozen pond. (sk, sc)

3. Each boy wore a heavy jacket, a _____arf, and mittens. (sc, sw)

4. Carson and Samir _____ent all afternoon at the pond. (sn, sp)

5. They even _____arted a game of hockey with a few friends. (st, sk)

6. Samir was careful not to _____ill the cocoa as he poured it from the thermos. (sc, sp)

7. The cocoa was _____eet and hot. It was a great way to end a busy day. (sm, sw)

Lesson 1.4 Beginning Two-Letter Blends with s

Underline the **s** blend in each word below. Then, draw a line to match each word with another word that begins with the same **s** blend.

1. scar		snarl
2. skunk		spy
3. smear		skirt
4. sneeze		stiff
5. spaceship		swamp
6. stare		scout
7. sweep		smack

Read the paragraphs below. On each line, write a word from the box that has an **s** blend. The words you choose should make sense in the sentences. You will use one word twice.

sky	smoke	skills	sniff	special	spark	stop	swiftly

Wildfires can be very dangerous. It is the job of firefighters to _____ the fires from spreading. They wear _____ gear to protect them from _____. These brave men and women work hard to keep the fires under control. They _____ the air and scan the _____ above the forest for signs of _____. They must act _____. Even a single _____ from a campfire can start a wildfire. If the fire becomes very large, as many as 10,000 firefighters might have to work together!

Fighting a wildfire is hard, hot, and dangerous. But most firefighters love their jobs. They like the excitement, and they know that their _____ can save people's lives.

Lesson 1.5 Beginning Two-Letter Blends with l

Some blends are made with **l** plus another consonant. Each of the words below has an **l** blend.

blank   **cl**ap   **fl**ash   **gl**ad   **pl**ace   **sl**eep

Say each picture name to yourself. Write the name of the picture on the line. Then, circle the **l** blend.

Read each meaning below. Choose a word from the box that matches the meaning. Write the word on the line.

| closet   slow   cloud   flea   blackboard   planets   glue |

1. _____ Mars, Jupiter, and Saturn are examples of this

2. _____ the opposite of *quick*

3. _____ a tiny insect that bites cats and dogs

4. _____ a white liquid used to stick two things together

5. _____ a puffy, white form in the sky

6. _____ a teacher uses chalk to write on this in a classroom

7. _____ a small room in which you keep your clothes

Lesson 1.5 Beginning Two-Letter Blends with l

Read the bold words below. Add **b, c, f, g, p,** or **s** to the beginning of each word to form as many new words as you can. Write the **l** blend words you formed on the lines.

lock   **lip**   **low**

_____ _____   _____ _____   _____ _____

_____   _____ _____   _____ _____

                                                                   _____

Read the sentences below. Circle the word with an **l** blend in each sentence. Then, think of another word that starts with the same blend. Write it on the line.

1. Jessy, Lena, and Cesar have a clubhouse in Lena's backyard. _____

2. The three friends were glad when Lena's dad said he'd help them build it. _____

3. The house is blue with a yellow door and yellow shutters. _____

4. A cheerful striped rug covers the wooden floor inside. _____

5. Jessy and Cesar made a special flag that hangs outside the front door. _____

6. Jessy climbed to the top of a stepladder to hang it. _____

7. On Saturday nights, their parents let them sleep in the little house. _____

8. The member made a secret pledge. _____

Lesson 1.6 Beginning Two-Letter Blends with r

Some blends are made with **r** plus another consonant. Each of the words below has an **r** blend.

brake   **cr**aft   **dr**eam   **fr**ee   **gr**een   **pr**ess   **tr**ick

Read the paragraphs below. Circle the 12 words that begin with an **r** blend.

The California Gold Rush began in 1848. A man found a nugget of gold in a river. His find drew thousands of people to Gold Country. They came from all over the world to try their luck.

Many people dreamed of growing rich. All they needed was a shovel and a large pan. Miners dug up gravel from creeks, lakes, and rivers. They shook their pans and hoped to see a bit of bright, shiny gold at the bottom. Some riverbeds were rich with gold. A lucky miner might make 1,000 dollars in one day. Other miners worked for weeks without a profit. Would you have traveled across the country for the promise of gold?

Read the sentences below. On each line, write an **r** blend from the pair in parentheses ( ). The word you form should make sense in the sentence.

1. A nickname for the _____owds moving west was "49ers" because many left home in 1849. (fr, cr)

2. On the _____ail to California, water was hard to get. (tr, pr)

3. Some people _____ossing the desert paid 100 dollars for a cup of water! (fr, cr)

4. There was _____eat excitement each time someone struck it rich. (gr, dr)

5. Mining companies _____illed deep tunnels in the hills to search for gold. (dr, gr)

6. Today, you can pan for shiny _____ains of gold at parks all over the country. (gr, tr)

Lesson 1.6 Beginning Two-Letter Blends with r

Underline the **r** blend in each word below. Then, draw a line to match each word with another word that begins with the same **r** blend.

1. graze		brain
2. frost		truth
3. brave		droop
4. crow		grade
5. tractor		craft
6. drain		practice
7. pretzel		Friday

Read each meaning below. Choose a word from the box that matches the meaning. Write the word on the line.

principal	crawl	broom	grandfather	crib
price	trash	green	friend	breakfast

1. _____ your mother's father

2. _____ the amount something costs

3. _____ the color of grass

4. _____ a pal or buddy

5. _____ something you use to sweep the floor

6. _____ a baby's bed

7. _____ the first meal you eat every day

8. _____ the head of a school

9. _____ garbage

10. _____ to move around on your hands and knees

NAME _____

Review   Two-Letter Blends

Look at the pictures and read the words. Circle the word that names each picture.

| snake | skate | freed | bleed | gloom | swoop |
| slate | brake | dread | bread | spoon | scoop |

| clam | claw | grump | brim | sky | fly |
| gram | draw | club | drum | try | sly |

Read the words in the box. Then, write them under the correct heading. Hint: Words that begin with **sl** can be placed under the **s-blend** and **l-blend** heading.

| plum | fruit | pretty | snail | trunk | smoky | scooter | slime |
| cry | slipper | drop | blaze | floppy | bring | skunk | glass |

s blend   **l** blend   **r** blend

_____   _____   _____

_____   _____   _____

_____   _____   _____

_____   _____   _____

_____   _____   _____

Review Two-Letter Blends

Read the tongue twisters below. One blend is used several times in each tongue twister. Find the blend and circle it each time it is used. Then, think of another word that begins with that blend, and write it on the line.

1. Blackbirds like blueberries better than bluebirds like blackberries. _____

2. Mrs. Clump's class clapped when the clumsy clown climbed the cliff. _____

3. The French frog is friends with five fellows named *Frank*. _____

4. The skillful skunk knows how to ski, skate, skip, sketch, and skateboard. _____

5. The cricket and the crane crunched crispy crackers by the creek. _____

6. The speedy spider spun a sparkly web in space. _____

7. The train traveled through traffic with a troop of trucks and tractors. _____

Now, choose a beginning blend and write a tongue twister of your own.

_____

_____

_____

_____

_____

Lesson 1.7 Beginning Three-Letter Blends

Some words begin with three consonants. Blend the sounds of the consonants together when you say the words. Each of the words below starts with a three-letter blend.

scrape   **spl**it   **spr**ing   **str**ipe

Read each word in bold. Circle the three-letter blend. Then, underline the word beside it that has the same blend.

1. **screen**	strike	scream	scold
2. **straight**	stray	sprout	splinter
3. **spray**	strong	scrape	spring
4. **split**	spine	splash	streak
5. **stream**	scratch	straw	sprain
6. **scrub**	scrap	scoop	strain

Read the paragraphs below. On each line, write a three-letter blend from the box. The word you form should make sense in the sentence.

scr	spl	spr	str

Addison and Luke Wallace found a _____ay cat in their yard. She had gray and white _____ipes and pretty green eyes. Mrs. Wallace helped them _____ub some old cat food dishes so they could feed her.

"She looks friendly," said Mrs. Wallace, "but she is still a _____ange cat. I want you both to be careful not to get _____atched."

The Wallaces made a cozy bed out of some fresh _____aw from the barn. They _____ead an old blanket over the straw. When Luke gave the cat some milk, she _____ashed in it with her paw. Then she licked the milk off her paw. Finally, she _____etched, curled up in a ball, and went to sleep.

Addison laughed. "I guess she feels right at home here!"

Lesson 1.7 Beginning Three-Letter Blends

Look at each picture and the word below it. The word that names the picture will begin with a three-letter blend (**scr**, **spl**, **str**, or **spr**). It will rhyme with the word in bold. Write the word on the line.

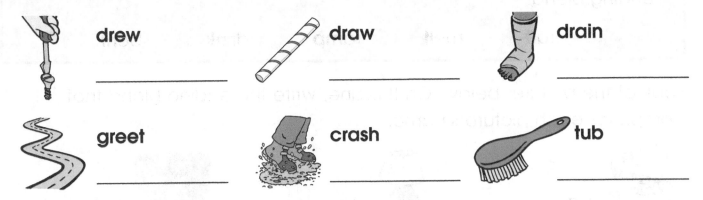

drew _____

draw _____

drain _____

greet _____

crash _____

tub _____

Read the clues below. On the line, write the word that matches each clue. The number of letters in each word is in parentheses ( ) at the end of the sentence. Remember, each word will start with one of these three-letter blends: **scr**, **spl**, **str**, or **spr**.

1. I'm used to water a lawn. Kids like to run through me on a hot day. (9 letters) _____

2. I am the season that comes between winter and summer. (6 letters) _____

3. I am another word for *yell*. (6 letters) _____

4. I am a sweet summer fruit. I am a red berry with tiny seeds and a green stem. Some people make jam out of me. (10 letters) _____

5. I am what you do when you have an itch. (7 letters) _____

6. I am powerful. I am a word that means the opposite of *weak*. (6 letters) _____

7. I am another word for *road*. Cars drive on me. (6 letters) _____

Lesson 1.8 Ending Blends

Some blends come at the ends of words. Blend the two consonants together when you say the words. Each of the words below has an ending blend.

craft   **melt**   **ramp**   **drink**   **bent**

Look at the pictures below. On the Line, write the ending blend that completes each picture's name.

pai_____   la_____   qui_____

chipmu_____   gi_____   ju_____

Read the sentences below. Circle the ending blends (**ft**, **lt**, **mp**, **nk**, **nt**) you find in each sentence.

1. Mr. Flores is a scientist who works with a chimp named Moe.

2. Mr. Flores is trying to learn how animals think.

3. Moe cannot talk, but Mr. Flores spent a long time teaching him sign language.

4. Whenever Mr. Flores felt that Moe earned a reward, he gave him a plump banana.

5. Moe learned to make signs for words like drink, soft, sleep, want, and funny.

6. When Moe signs a word correctly, he jumps for joy.

7. "You're a champ, Moe," cheers Mr. Flores.

Lesson 1.8 Ending Blends

Read each sentence and the set of words that follows it. Choose the word that best completes the sentence and write it on the line. Then, circle the ending blend.

1. Next weekend, we are going to _____ at the Blue Spruce State Park. (camp, damp, colt)

2. We'll sleep in our new, three-room _____. (rent, tank, tent)

3. Dad said that we'll set up camp on a bed of _____ pine needles. (sift, soft, salt)

4. I can't wait to _____ down Spruce River. (raft, rank, craft)

5. My sister, Linh, is worried the raft will _____. (wink, sent, sink)

6. My uncle _____ us some lifejackets, so now Linh is excited too. (lent, tint, lamp)

7. At night, we'll _____ cocoa and roast marshmallows. (dunk, drink, drift)

8. I like my marshmallows _____ to a crisp on the outside. (bent, shift, burnt)

9. Last night, I _____ so excited I could hardly sleep. (felt, front, blink)

10. I just hope we don't get sprayed by a _____ like my grandpa did the last time he went camping! (slump, skunk, trunk)

Lesson 1.9 More Ending Blends

Some blends come at the ends of words. Blend the two consonants together when you say the words. Each of the words below has an ending blend.

chi**ld**   ba**nd**   de**sk**   be**st**

On the line, write the ending blend (**ld**, **nd**, **sk**, **st**) that completes each picture's name.

 ba_____

 sa_____

 de_____

 ca_____

ma_____

fi_____

 ha_____

Find each picture name in the word search puzzle. Circle each word you find.

ne_____

shie_____

c	a	s	t	l	r	b	u	p
g	n	d	d	i	h	a	n	d
q	e	g	n	b	o	l	j	o
z	s	h	i	e	l	d	a	t
d	t	v	t	u	a	s	f	b
e	r	f	l	v	i	n	i	r
s	a	n	d	h	m	a	s	k
k	o	u	l	f	d	n	t	y

Lesson 1.9 More Ending Blends

Read each word in bold. Circle the ending blend. Then, underline the word beside it that has the same blend.

1. **wrist**	risk	roast	wild
2. **dusk**	build	send	ask
3. **mold**	field	blind	sound
4. **stand**	child	grind	post
5. **just**	task	east	sold
6. **unfold**	held	hound	twist
7. **wand**	trust	disk	and
8. **task**	ask	wind	billfold

Read each meaning below. Choose a word from the box that matches the meaning. Write the word on the line.

blend	cold	mask	band	dentist	toast	old	west	gold	disk

1. _____ a doctor who takes care of your teeth

2. _____ the direction that is the opposite of *east*

3. _____ something you put over your face as a costume

4. _____ a group of people who make music together

5. _____ to mix together

6. _____ the opposite of *young*

7. _____ a very valuable yellow metal

8. _____ a shiny, round piece of plastic used to store music or computer files

9. _____ chilly; not warm

10. _____ slices of lightly cooked bread

Review Three-Letter Blends and Ending Blends

Look at each picture below. On the first line, write the word that names the picture. Circle the ending blend. Now, choose a word from the box that has the same ending blend. Write it on the second line.

left	crust	amount	salt	honk	dump

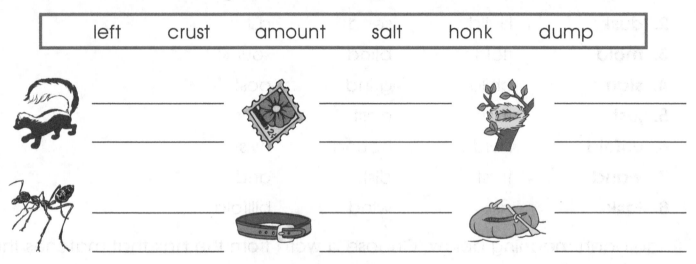

Read the story below. Find the 14 words that begin with a three-letter blend (**scr**, **spl**, **spr**, **str**). Circle each word you find.

On Saturday night, we had strawberry shortcake for dessert. I split a big piece with my brother, Drew. The whole family sat outside on the screened porch. We watched people stroll down the street. All of a sudden, we heard something strange. There was a low, buzzing sound all around us. My brother sprang out of his chair, and his shortcake splattered on the ground.

"Mosquitoes!" screamed Drew, as he sprinted inside. Dozens of mosquitoes streamed in through a small tear in one of the screens. I started to scratch just looking at them.

"Everyone inside," said Mom. She scraped up the shortcake from the ground. "I guess we found out what mosquitoes like best for dessert," she said with a laugh.

Review Three-Letter Blends and Ending Blends

Read the paragraphs below. The words in bold are not complete. Complete the words by choosing an ending blend from the pair in parentheses ( ) and writing it on the line. The words you form should make sense in the sentences.

Every autumn, you probably see hundreds of acorns on the **grou**_____ (nd, ld). Acorns are the fruit of oak trees. **Wi**_____ (mp, ld) animals, like birds, squirrels, bears, **a**_____ (sk, nd) deer, eat these little nuts. But did you ever **thi**_____ (nk, nt) that people could eat acorns too? Native Americans used acorns in many ways. They could **gri**_____ (ld, nd) the nuts to make acorn flour, or they could boil and **roa**_____ (st, sk) them. **Mo**_____ (lt, st) acorns are bitter, so they are not eaten raw.

If you **wa**_____ (nt, nd) to prepare acorns at home, collect some **rou**_____ (nd, mp), **plu**_____ (st, mp) acorns. They should not be **so**_____ (lt, ft) or have any holes or cracks. Use a nutcracker to get the nut out of the shell. Put the nuts in a pot with water **a**_____ (nd, st) boil them. When the water turns **almo**_____ (st, ft) brown, change it. Keep doing this until the water doesn't change color. Then, bake the acorns at a low heat for about two hours. You can sprinkle **sa**_____ (lt, nk) on them **a**_____ (mp, nd) eat them for a tasty snack.

Lesson 1.10 Beginning Digraphs

A **digraph** is a combination of two letters that stand for one sound. You do not hear the sound of each letter in a digraph. Instead, the letters form a new sound.

- The digraph **sh** makes the sound you hear in **sh**ee*t*, **sh**o*p*, and **sh**y.

- The digraph **ch** makes the sound you hear in **ch**i*ld*, **ch**i*n*, and **ch**e*ckers*.

Look at each picture below. On the first line, write the word that names the picture. Circle the digraph. Now, think of another word that has the same digraph. Write it on the second line.

Read the clues below. On the line, write the word that matches each clue. Remember, each word will start with a digraph.

1. I am the opposite of *dull*. You need to be careful with me so you don't get cut. _____

2. I am an animal that lives in the ocean. I have a large fin on my back. Many people are afraid of me. _____

3. I am the opposite of *expensive*. _____

4. I am part of your face. You can find me below your mouth. _____

Lesson 1.10 Beginning Digraphs

Read the words below. One word in each set does not belong. Underline the digraph of the word that does not belong in the set.

1. shallow   child   shave
2. shine   charm   chime
3. shin   shot   chip
4. shawl   shelf   choose
5. cherry   shower   chilly
6. shade   checker   chant

Read the sentences below. Complete each incomplete word with the digraph **sh** or **ch**.

1. Devon loves to bake _____ocolate _____ip cookies with his grandma.

2. After school, Diana and her mom will go _____opping for new

    _____oes.

3. Please don't _____ange the _____annel until there is an ad.

4. "Did you see the _____ark?" _____outed Bridget.

5. _____ould we _____ovel the snow this afternoon?

6. Maria never _____eats when she plays _____ess.

7. I need to find the _____ampoo before I take a _____ower.

8. The baker made three _____erry _____eesecakes.

9. Would you like _____eese on your _____icken sandwich?

10. Deepak _____owed Leo how to float in the _____allow end of the pool.

Lesson 1.11 More Beginning Digraphs

Remember that a **digraph** is a combination of two letters that stand for one sound.

- The digraph **th** can make the sound you hear in **th***orn* and **th***ing*. It can also make the sound you hear in **th***at* and **th***ey*.
- The digraph **wh** can make the /hw/ sound you hear in **wh***y* and **wh***isper*. It can also make the /h/ sound you hear in **wh***o* and **wh***ole*.
- The digraph **ph** makes the /f/ sound you hear in **ph***one* and **ph***onics*.

Look at each picture below. On the first line, write the word that names the picture. Circle the digraph. Now, think of another word that has the same digraph. Write it on the second line.

Read each word in bold. Circle the digraph. Then, circle the word beside it that has the same beginning sound. If you are not sure, say the words out loud. Hint: The sounds can be the same even when the spellings are different. (Example: *phase* and *fancy*)

1. **thirteen**	them	thief	while
2. **that**	third	phonics	these
3. **what**	thought	wheat	thanks
4. **phew**	photo	whip	poster
5. **thirsty**	those	phony	thumb
6. **whisk**	throw	water	whose
7. **whom**	when	happy	thick
8. **phrase**	fresh	thimble	pink

Lesson 1.11 More Beginning Digraphs

Read the story below. Circle each word that begins with the digraph **th**. Underline words that begin with **wh**. Draw a box around words that begin with **ph**. Note: The name *Phoebe* is pronounced *fee bee*.

Philip was a handsome white whale. He weighed thousands of pounds, but he was still a graceful swimmer. As Philip swam in giant circles, he thought about what it would be like to have a friend. All the fish in the ocean thought that Philip was too big to play with. He was lonely.

One day, Philip was taking a nap in the sun when he heard a tiny whisper. "Who's there?" asked the whale, opening one huge eye. There were three tiny birds sitting on his forehead.

"I'm Theo," said one. "These are my sisters, Bella and Phoebe."

"How wonderful to have sisters!" said Philip. "Whatever you do, you always have two friends."

"We have three more sisters at home," said Theo. "I'd show you a photo, but it's a little wet here."

"I'm very glad to meet you, of course," said Philip. "But what are you doing in the middle of the ocean?"

"We're looking for adventure," said Phoebe. "We want to make friends and see the whole world. Do you think you might like to join us?"

Philip laughed. He thumped his giant whale tail. He whistled through his blowhole. "I can't think of anything I'd like better!"

Lesson 1.12 Ending Digraphs

Some digraphs, like **sh**, **ch**, **th**, and **ph** can also come at the ends of words.

pu**sh**   bea**ch**   wi**th**   gra**ph**

Read each meaning below. Choose the word from the box that matches the meaning. Write the word on the line.

| lunch   teeth   brush   watch   match   north   leash   photograph |

1. _____ a small clock you wear on your wrist

2. _____ what you do every day to your teeth and your hair

3. _____ a picture taken with a camera

4. _____ the meal between breakfast and dinner

5. _____ the opposite of south

6. _____ a long cord or strap used when walking a dog

7. _____ something used to light a candle or start a fire

8. _____ the white things in your mouth used for chewing

Read the sentences below. One ending digraph is used several times in each sentence. Find the digraph and circle it each time it is used. Then, think of another word that ends with that digraph and write it in the blank.

1. _____ Each of the kids ate a sandwich and a peach for lunch.

2. _____ I wish you would wash that dish before you mash the potatoes.

3. _____ Both of the Cohen boys are in the fifth grade and love math and hockey.

Lesson 1.12 Ending Digraphs

On the line, write the ending digraph that completes each picture's name.

wrea_____   **th** digra_____   fi_____

wat_____   bu_____   pa_____

tableclo_____   autogra_____   ben_____

Find each picture name in the word search puzzle. Circle the words you find.

t	a	b	l	e	c	l	o	t	h
k	u	u	r	e	n	t	l	p	u
o	t	s	v	j	b	a	c	a	n
w	o	h	h	f	d	n	s	t	n
q	g	r	t	i	z	f	q	h	b
x	r	y	t	s	y	s	p	a	e
w	a	t	c	h	o	s	r	d	n
i	p	u	w	r	e	a	t	h	c
l	h	f	d	i	g	r	a	p	h

Lesson 1.13 More Ending Digraphs

Other digraphs, like **ck**, **ng**, and **gh**, can also come at the ends of words.
- The digraph **ck** makes the /k/ sound in sa**ck** and thi**ck**.
- The digraph **ng** makes the ending sound in ha**ng** and you**ng**.
- The digraph **gh** can make the /f/ sound in tou**gh** and enou**gh**.

Circle the word that names each picture below.

duck   sink   laugh
dunk   swing   lock

wick   tough   sock
wing   truck   song

Read the sentences below. Some words are not complete. Add **ck**, **ng**, or **gh** to form the word or words that best complete each sentence.

1. Next week, Alex is goi_____ to compete in a spelling bee.

2. He has made it to the finals, so he knows the words will be tou_____.

3. Before he leaves, Alex wants to che_____ his backpa_____ for his dictionary and flashcards.

4. He doesn't want to spell a word wro_____ because he didn't study hard enou_____.

5. Alex is you_____, but he has been traini_____ for a lo_____ time.

6. Sometimes, learni_____ the meani_____ of a word can help Alex spell it.

7. As Alex spells his words, he hears the ti_____ of the clo_____ and hopes the buzzer doesn't ri_____.

Lesson 1.13 More Ending Digraphs

Read the paragraphs below. Complete the words by choosing an ending digraph from the pair in parentheses ( ) and writing it on the line. The words you form should make sense in the sentences.

Have you ever heard of a triathlon? It is a tou_____ (ck, gh) race of swimmi_____ (ng, ck), runni_____ (gh, ng), and biki_____ (ck, ng). The most famous race is called the Ironman Triathlon. It takes place in Hawaii. The athletes must swim more than 2 miles, bike 112 miles, and run 26 miles. Not all triathlons are this lo_____ (ng, gh). Even kids can compete in the Ironkids Triathlon.

Traini_____ (gh, ng) for a race can be harder than people expect. A little bit of lu_____ (ck, ng) isn't enou_____ (ck, gh). The athletes spend lots of time at the tra_____ (ng, ck), in the pool, and on bike trails. They are always racing against the clo_____ (ck, gh). Some belo_____ (gh, ng) to clubs. Others choose to blo_____ (ng, ck) everythi_____ (ng, ck) out and work on their own.

One thing is for sure: After finishi_____ (ng, ck) a race, the athletes know they can do anythi_____ (gh, ng)!

Now, write the words you completed on the lines beside the correct headings.

ck: _____ _____ _____ _____

ng: _____ _____ _____ _____ _____

_____ _____ _____

gh: _____ _____

Lesson 1.14 Silent Consonants

> In some consonant pairs, one letter is silent.
> - The letters **kn** can make the /n/ sound you hear in **kn**ot and **kn**ee. The **k** is silent.
> - The letters **wr** can make the /r/ sound you hear in **wr**ap and **wr**ong. The **w** is silent.
> - The letters **sc** can make the /s/ sound you hear iin **sc**ience and **sc**ene. The **c** is silent.

Look at each picture, and read the word beside it. Change the letter or letters in bold to **kn**, **wr**, or **sc** so that the word names the picture. Write the new word on the line.

trot _____ **tw**inkle _____ **br**ight _____

Read each word in bold. Circle the word beside it that has the same beginning sound. If you are not sure, say the words out loud.

Hint: Two sounds can be the same even when the spellings are different. (Example: *knit* and *nice*)

1. **knock**   kick   never   kid
2. **wrestle** wrinkle   west   Wednesday
3. **science** cute   scissors   shop
4. **knew**   wren   king   knob
5. **scene**   seven   scare   crumb
6. **wrist**   wild   wrapper   whisper
7. **knead**   nest   kiss   wreath
8. **wrote**   wire   knock   rail

Lesson 1.14 Silent Consonants

Read each sentence below. Then, read the pair of words that follow. On the line, write the word that best completes each sentence.

1. Amelia loves to read and hopes to be a _____ when she grows up. (writer, wrapper)

2. _____ the dough until it feels soft and stretchy. (Knit, Knead)

3. José's brother is on the _____ team. (wrestling, wrinkle)

4. I love the _____ of cinnamon and apples in the air when we bake a pie. (scent, science)

5. Carter _____ what time the bus will come. (kneel, knows)

6. Bakari's aunt is a _____ who works with dangerous materials. (scientist, scissors)

7. Grandma _____ me two sweaters for my birthday. (knew, knit)

8. The students in Ms. Hopple's class made autumn _____ out of dried leaves and branches. (wreaths, wrecks)

Read each meaning below. Choose a word from the box that matches the meaning. Write the word on the line.

knock	scent	wrong	wrap	scissors	knight

1. _____ not correct; the opposite of *right*

2. _____ a smell

3. _____ a soldier from long ago who fought wearing heavy armor

4. _____ two blades that are used for cutting; they come in pairs

5. _____ to cover a gift with colorful paper

Lesson 1.15 More Silent Consonants

When two or three consonants appear together, one letter is sometimes silent.

- The letters **mb** can make the /m/ sound you hear in *thu**mb*** and *li**mb***. The **b** is silent.
- The letters **tch** can make the /ch/ sound you hear in *ha**tch*** and *pi**tch***. The **t** is silent.

In some pairs, both letters are silent.

- The letters **gh** can be silent in the middle or end of a word, as in *li**gh**t* and *wei**gh***.

Look at each picture. The letters beside the picture are scrambled. Unscramble them to form a word that matches the picture. Write the word on the line. Hint: Each word contains **mb**, **tch**, or **gh**.

tcaheth

_____

hesgli

_____

cprtihe

_____

laghftlshi

_____

hesrtct

_____

umthb

_____

sthopcoch

_____

lbam

_____

ihngt

_____

bmoc

_____

curcth

_____

gstolipht

_____

Lesson 1.15 More Silent Consonants

Read each word below. Find a rhyming word in the box and write it on the line. Then, cross out the letter or letters that are silent.

lamb scratch climb sleigh limb stitch straight comb flight thumb

1. _____ come
2. _____ way
3. _____ slim
4. _____ fright
5. _____ batch

6. _____ dome
7. _____ dime
8. _____ hate
9. _____ rich
10. _____ Sam

Choose the word from the box that best completes each sentence below. Write it on the line.

might   crumbs   sunlight   sight   limb   sketch   itches

1. Max will use his new colored pencils to _____ the birds in his yard.

2. First, he puts out some _____ to attract the birds.

3. He tries to stay out of _____ so that he does not scare them away.

4. Max _____ a bug bite and wishes the birds would snack on the backyard bugs.

5. If it weren't for the bugs, Max _____ stay outside and draw all day long.

6. The yard is filled with _____, and Max starts to draw two blue jays playing in the birdbath.

7. He stops for a minute to sketch a bright red cardinal sitting on a

_____ of the cherry tree.

Review Digraphs and Silent Consonants

Remember, a **digraph** is a combination of two letters that stand for one sound. Together, the letters form a new sound. Some digraphs come at the beginnings of words. Others come at the ends of words. **Sh, th, ck**, and **ng** are examples of digraphs.

ship	**th**imble	sti**ck**	si**ng**

Read each clue below. In the blank, write the word that matches the clue. Each word will begin or end with one of these digraphs: **sh, ch, th, wh, ph, ck, ng, gh**.

1. You hear me during a storm. I make loud booms and crashes in the sky. ____ ____ ____ ____ ____ ____ ____

2. I am the number that comes between twelve and fourteen.

   ____ ____ ____ ____ ____ ____ ____ ____

3. People eat me for lunch. I am made with two slices of bread and some filling. ____ ____ ____ ____ ____ ____ ____ ____

4. I am fluffy and white. Wool is made from my fur. I make this sound: *baaaaa*. ____ ____ ____ ____ ____

5. I wear a crown. A queen is my partner. ____ ____ ____ ____

6. I am a dark color. I am the opposite of *white*. ____ ____ ____ ____ ____

7. I am what a person does when something is funny.

   ____ ____ ____ ____ ____

8. You can use me to call people. When you have a call, I make a ringing noise. ____ ____ ____ ____ ____

Review Digraphs and Silent Consonants

Read the paragraphs below. Complete the words by choosing letters from the pair in parentheses ( ). The words you form should make sense in the sentences.

Benjamin Franklin was a printer, an inventor, a _____iter (kn, wr), and

a _____ientist (sh, sc). When he was you_____ (th, ng), Franklin owned his

own printing _____op (wh, sh). He printed newspapers and a popular

book called Poor Richard's Almana_____ (ck, ng).

Ben Franklin loved books and helped set up the first public library in

America. He was also known as one of the Foundi_____ (ng, ck) Fathers of

our country. His autogra_____ (gh, ph) is on the Declaration of

Independence and the Constitution. He fou_____t (gh, th) against things,

like slavery, that he _____ew (kn, wr) were _____ong (wr, sc). Some

people _____ink (sh, th) he was ahead of his time.

Franklin proved that li_____tning (gh, ph) is a form of electricity. Later,

he invented the lightni_____ (ck, ng) rod. He also invented the wood

stove, swim fins, and a new type of glasses that helped people with bad

eyesi_____t (th, gh).

Franklin was an amazi_____ (ng, ck) person. _____at (Wh, Th) would

you ask him if he were still alive today?

Did You Know? Some words change their spelling over time. Today, the
word *almanac* ends with a **c**. In Ben Franklin's day, it was spelled with a
ck (almanack). Do you know any old-fashioned spellings for other words?

Lesson 1.16 Short Vowels

> The letter **a** can make the short vowel sound you hear in words like *snap* and *tan*.

Look at the pictures and read the words below. Circle the word that names each picture.

trash wrap pan   last tank sang   sad raft clam

    4+6=10

fact fan stack   cab lamp slap   rat bank math

Read the sentences below. Underline each word that has a short **a** sound. The number at the end of the sentence will tell you how many short a words you should find.

1. Cass and Matt would like to get three fish tanks. (4)

2. They made a plan, and they saved some cash. (3)

3. Mrs. Grant drove Cass and Matt to the bank and the pet shop. (6)

4. The man at the shop held a scoop in his hand, and the Grants told him which fish to catch. (6)

5. He asked them if they needed a batch of plants and some fish food. (4)

6. Back at home, Cass and Matt found the perfect place for their new tank. (5)

7. They named the fish Dan, Sam, and Max. Wait till the fish find out the Grants own two cats! (6)

Lesson 1.16 Short Vowels

> The letter **e** can make the short vowel sound you hear in words like *help* and *cent*.

Look at each picture below. On the line, write the word that names the picture.

Read the clues below. Write the answers in the numbered spaces in the crossword puzzle. Each correct answer will have the short **e** sound.

Across

3. to fix something broken or torn; rhymes with *send*
5. a place to store your book; rhymes with *elf*
6. the opposite of *dry*
7. a piece of leather worn around the waist

Down

1. the number after *nine*
2. you use your nose to do this; it is one of the five senses
4. the place where birds lay their eggs
6. the opposite of *east*

Lesson 1.16 Short Vowels

> The letter **i** can make the short vowel sound you hear in words like *chimp* and *fill*.

Look at each picture. Write the word that names the picture on the line. It will rhyme with the word in bold.

pick

_____

rib

_____

drip

_____

sniff

_____

spill

_____

grins

_____

Read the sentences below. On each line, write a word from the pair in parentheses ( ). The word you choose should make sense in the sentence.

1. _____ (Big, Bring) Ben is the name of a famous clock tower and bell in London.

2. The hour bell weighs almost 14 tons and fills the air with a loud
_____ (limping, ringing) sound.

3. A team of 16 horses _____ (spilled, hitched) to a wagon pulled the bell to the tower in 1858.

4. The clock has been in many _____ (films, kicks).

5. The tower is _____ (thick, lit) up against London's night sky.

6. In October 2005, the hands of the clock were _____ (skid, still) for 33 hours.

7. Even with heavy _____ (wind, cliff), snow, and storms, the clock does not break down often.

Lesson 1.16 Short Vowels

The letter **o** can make the short vowel sound you hear in words like *chop* and *dog*.

Look at the pictures and read the words below. Circle the word that names each picture.

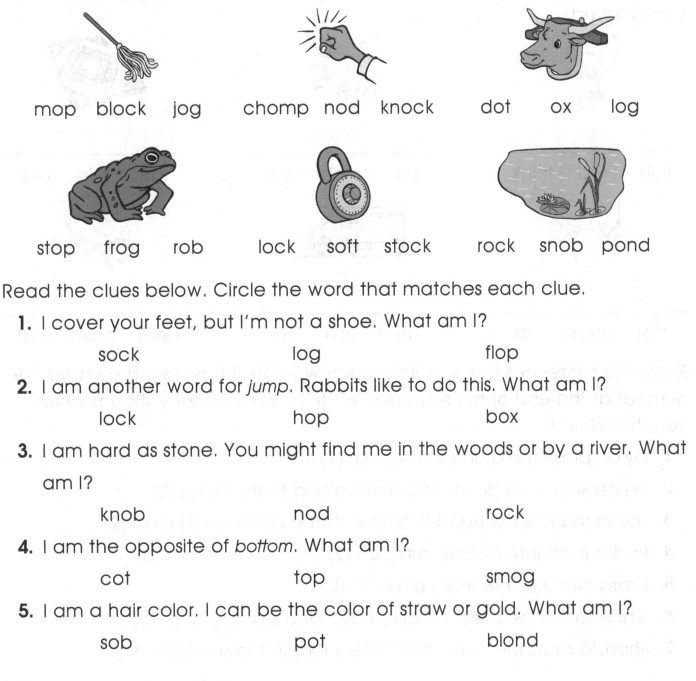

mop   block   jog   chomp   nod   knock   dot   ox   log

stop   frog   rob   lock   soft   stock   rock   snob   pond

Read the clues below. Circle the word that matches each clue.

1. I cover your feet, but I'm not a shoe. What am I?

      sock   log   flop

2. I am another word for *jump*. Rabbits like to do this. What am I?

      lock   hop   box

3. I am hard as stone. You might find me in the woods or by a river. What am I?

      knob   nod   rock

4. I am the opposite of *bottom*. What am I?

      cot   top   smog

5. I am a hair color. I can be the color of straw or gold. What am I?

      sob   pot   blond

Lesson 1.16 Short Vowels

The letter **u** can make the short vowel sound you hear in words like *dug* and *plum*.

Look at the pictures and read the words below. On the line, write the word that names the picture. Then, circle the word that has the same short vowel sound.

_____   _____   _____

fluff   Fred   think   sat   lunch   left   ham   thin   junk

_____   _____   _____

plot   scrub   kiss   mud   job   hip   dent   part   dust

Read the sentences below. Circle each word that has a short **u** sound. The number at the end of the sentence will tell you how many short **u** words you should find.

1. Dylan plays the drums in a band. (1)
2. Simon strums his guitar and hums along to the tune. (2)
3. Thalia thumps her hand in time with the drummer's beat. (2)
4. Pedro puffs into a shiny trumpet. (2)
5. Clara clutches her trusty clarinet. (2)
6. Chelsea chugs a cup of fruit punch and starts to sing. (3)
7. Shonda shuts the door, and Peter plugs in the speakers. (2)

NAME _____

Lesson 1.16 Short Vowels

Read the paragraphs below. Each of the words in bold has a short vowel sound. Listen to the vowel sound and write each word in bold under the correct heading. An example has been added below each heading to help you.

Have you ever heard of the author Eve Bunting? She **has** written more **than** 150 books for **kids**. She writes about many different **things** that are important to her in some way. Eve has written about animals, like **ducks** and **dogs**. She has written about mummies, the **Civil** War, and growing **up** in Ireland. She has even written a book about the great **ship** *Titanic*.

When Eve **visits** classes, students have **lots** of questions for her. Many of **them** want to know where she **gets** her ideas. Eve **tells** them that an idea might hit her anywhere. For example, she **got** the idea to write her **mummy** book after a **trip** to the museum.

Eve has said that she likes to write books **that** make children **ask** questions. If you think you might like to try an Eve Bunting book, **check** your library. It is sure to have many books by this popular writer.

short a	short e	short i	short o	short u
cap	pet	kick	stop	snug

Lesson 1.17 Long Vowel Sounds

> The letter **a** can make a long sound, as in *cake*, when it is followed by a consonant and silent **e**. Sometimes, this pattern is called *VCe*. That stands for *Vowel + Consonant + Silent* **e**. The silent **e** makes the vowel say its name.

The words in bold all have the short **a** sound. Add silent **e** to each word and write the new word on the line. Then, draw a line to match each new word to a rhyming word in the second column.

1. **cap** + **e** = _____   sale

2. **sam** + **e** = _____   plane

3. **man** + **e** = _____   cage

4. **past** + **e** = _____   tape

5. **hat** + **e** = _____   came

6. **mad** + **e** = _____   fade

7. **pal** + **e** = _____   taste

8. **rag** + **e** = _____   rate

Read each word in bold below. Underline the world beside that has the same long vowel sound.

1. **shade**	sharp	wage	cast
2. **space**	lamp	call	quake
3. **whale**	vane	champ	saggy
4. **flake**	dark	past	vase
5. **blame**	band	cave	tax
6. **crate**	waste	splat	crack

Lesson 1.17 Long Vowel Sounds

The letter **i** can make a long sound, as in *hide*, when it is followed by a consonant and silent **e**.

Read the silly sentences below. Circle each word that has the long **i** sound spelled **i-consonant-e**.

1. The little mice use a lot of spice when they make white rice.

2. If you dive at low tide, you can see creatures with spines, spikes, and stripes.

3. We will dine on a nice slice of lime that's ripe from the vine.

4. If you are wise, you will hike nine miles to see the sun rise.

5. The swine will glide and slide in the slime each time the weather is fine.

6. Wipe and shine each side of the shoes in the pile twice.

7. Let us fly five fine kites tied with twine.

8. The bride will glide for five miles while she skydives.

Read the long **i** words in the box. Write some silly sentences of your own. You can use other long **i** words if you like, but they should have the **i-consonant-e** spelling. You may use the words in the box more than once.

nice	crime	hide	ride	spike	stripe	white
write	hike	kite	mice	drive	five	nine

1. _____

2. _____

3. _____

4. _____

Lesson 1.17 Long Vowel Sounds

> • The letter **o** can make a long sound, as in *rope*, when it is followed by a consonant and silent **e**.
> • The letter **o** can also make a long sound when it is followed only by silent **e**, as in *Joe*.

Look at the pictures below. On the lines, write the words that name the pictures. Each picture name will have a long **o** sound.

Read the meanings below. On the lines, write the words from the box that match the meanings.

whole	home	doe	joke	mole	rose	Rome

1. _____ a female deer

2. _____ a small animal that lives underground

3. _____ a city in Italy

4. _____ something funny you tell other people

5. _____ another word for *house*

6. _____ a type of flower

7. _____ the opposite of *half*

Lesson 1.17 Long Vowel Sounds

- The letter **u** can make a long sound, as in *cute* or *rule*, when it is followed by a consonant and silent **e**.
- The letter **u** can also make a long sound when it is followed only by silent **e**, as in *due*.

Read each word in bold. Underline the word beside it that has the same long **u** sound. If you are not sure, say the words out loud.

1. **use**	dug	cube	cut
2. **tube**	tub	run	rude
3. **June**	plume	plum	truck
4. **glue**	jump	tune	thump
5. **rule**	dude	rug	hum
6. **fuse**	shut	cute	just
7. **mute**	must	fuse	much

Read the sentences below. On the line, write a long **u** word from the pair in parentheses ( ). The word you choose should make sense in the sentence.

1. Every _____ (June, cube), _____ (tune, Sue) prunes the lilac bushes in her yard.

2. One _____ (fume, rule) at the library is that you return books when they are _____ (sun, due).

3. Play me a pretty _____ (clue, tune) on your

   _____ (flute, dude).

4. Hannah's _____ (cute, cut), gray _____ (huge, mule) has long, soft ears.

5. Sayako found all the _____ (clues, dust), and now she's looking for the prize.

Lesson 1.17 Long Vowel Sounds

Look at each picture below. On the first line, write the word that names the picture. Then, think of another word that has the same long vowel sound. Write it on the second line.

Find each picture name in the word search puzzle. Circle each word you find.

r	y	c	a	k	e	g	h	l	g
d	u	q	b	b	w	a	j	o	l
b	p	s	c	e	h	r	f	n	u
l	t	v	p	l	a	t	e	s	e
h	w	u	c	n	l	c	e	d	a
b	h	r	o	s	e	r	p	i	x
b	j	k	n	c	e	o	l	c	f
n	i	n	e	s	b	i	k	e	t
h	n	d	a	j	y	q	d	e	z

Lesson 1.17 Long Vowel Sounds

Read the paragraphs below. Each of the words in bold has a long vowel sound. Listen to the vowel sound and write each word in bold under the correct heading. An example has been added below each heading to help you.

Does your **state** have a nickname? The story of a state's nickname can be a **clue** to its history. It tells you what the people who live there think is important about their **home**.

Florida is called the Sunshine State because the sun **shines** there all year long. Kentucky is the Bluegrass State. Bluegrass is actually green, but the buds are **blue**. They can **make** fields of grass look blue. Maine is known as the **Pine** Tree State. It has more than 17 million acres of forest!

Maryland goes by the **name** Old **Line** State. Some people think George Washington named Maryland for its line troops during the Revolutionary War.

One of Michigan's names is the Great **Lake** State. Michigan is **close** to four of the Great Lakes. There are thousands of smaller lakes around the state too.

Texas is the **Lone** Star State. There are a few different ideas about how Texas got its name. One thing is for sure—a single star has been on the Texas flag since before it was even a state.

If you could **vote** on a new nickname for your state, what would it be?

long **a**	long **i**	long **o**	long **u**
take	ride	zone	due
_____	_____	_____	_____
_____	_____	_____	_____
_____	_____	_____	_____
_____		_____	

Review Short and Long Vowel Sounds

Read each word in bold below. Decide whether the vowel sound is long or short and circle your choice.

1. rug	short	long		7. stomp	short	long
2. shape	short	long		8. made	short	long
3. stripe	short	long		9. patch	short	long
4. huge	short	long		10. rode	short	long
5. slim	short	long		11. dip	short	long
6. pet	short	long		12. up	short	long

A "hink pink" is a type of word game. Read each clue. The correct answer will be a pair of rhyming words from the box. Write the words on the first line. On the second line, write the vowel sound you hear in the words. The first one is done for you.

> cute flute   best nest   space place   hot pot
> twin grin   whale sale   mad dad

1. a container of boiling water _____hot pot_____ _____short o_____

2. an angry father _____ _____

3. a location that is out of this world _____ _____

4. the number one bird's home _____ _____

5. a good-looking instrument _____ _____

6. two smiles that are exactly the same _____

_____

7. a good price for huge underwater animals _____

_____

Review Short and Long Vowel Sounds

Read the recipe below. On the line next to the words in bold, write the long or short vowel sound you hear. Example: **Mix** _____*short i*_____ the ingredients together.

Banana Bread

2 cups flour

¾ teaspoon baking soda

½ teaspoon salt

1 **cup** _____ sugar

¼ cup butter

2 eggs

1½ cups **ripe** _____ banana

⅓ cup yogurt

1 teaspoon vanilla

½ teaspoon cinnamon

½ teaspoon **cloves** _____

½ cup **nuts** _____

- Heat the oven to 350°. Mix together the flour, baking soda, and salt. Stir **with** _____ a whisk. **Blend** _____ the sugar and butter in a large bowl. You can use a mixer, or you can do it by **hand** _____ Add the eggs, one at a **time** _____.

- Use a fork to **mash** _____ the bananas in another bowl. Add the bananas, yogurt, and **spices** _____. Mix well. **Then** _____, add the banana mixture to the flour mixture. Stir **just** _____ until moist.

- Coat a loaf **pan** _____ with butter or cooking spray. Put the batter in the pan. **Bake** _____ for one hour. If you insert a **pick** _____ into the center of the bread and it is clean, your bread is done. If it is gooey, the bread needs to keep baking.

- Cool the bread on a **wire** _____ **rack** _____. Serve it on a pretty **plate** _____ for breakfast or a snack.

Lesson 1.18 Vowel Sounds (ai, ay, ei)

- The letters **ai** can make the long **a** sound you hear in m**ai**d and br**ai**n.
- The letters **ay** can make the long **a** sound you hear in cl**ay** and spr**ay**.
- The letters **ei** can make the long **a** sound you hear in w**ei**gh and sl**ei**gh.

Read the clues below. Underline the word that matches each clue.

1. People use me to catch fish, but I'm not a fishing pole. What am I?

   play   bait   sleigh

2. I am the sound a horse makes. What am I?

   vein   neigh   sway

3. There are 365 of me every year. I am 24 hours long. What am I?

   vase   pain   day

4. I am a state in the Northeast. I am known for lobster. It gets very cold here in the winter. What am I?

   stay   Maine   Spain

5. Brides often wear me. I am usually white, and I cover the bride's face. What am I?

   veil   rain   tray

6. I am a type of bird. I am usually blue. I have a loud voice. What am I?

   flame   jay   skate

7. I wear my house on my back. What am I?

   gray   cape   snail

8. I am the number that comes between seven and nine. What am I?

   eight   play   laid

Lesson 1.18 Vowel Sounds (ai, ay, ei)

Read the paragraphs below. On each line, write a word from the pair in parentheses ( ). The word you choose should make sense in the sentence.

A rail _____ (trail, hay) can be a great place to bike, walk, or ride horses. _____ (Veil, Rail) trails used to be _____ (train, wait) tracks. Trains were the best way to send _____ (mail, sleigh) and heavy _____ (freight, clay) across the country. Over time, people started using trucks more than trains. Lots of old tracks that were no longer being used _____ (swayed, remained). Cities and states _____ (paid, grain) for the land and the tracks. They wanted to turn these areas into greenspace.

The first rail trail opened in Wisconsin in 1965. Since then, thousands of other trails have been _____ (rain, laid) from _____ (Maine, plain) to California. The longest one is in Missouri. It stretches about 200 miles!

People like rail trails because they are usually _____ (weigh, straight) and flat. Since they used to be train tracks, they are often near cities. If you would like to visit a rail trail near your home, you _____ (braid, may) want to check out this Web site: www.trailink.com. You'll find a great place to get _____ (away, pay) for the _____ (rain, day). Grab your bike, a friend, or the _____ (tray, reins) of a horse, and have fun.

Lesson 1.19 Vowel Sounds (ee, ea, ie)

- The letters **ee** make the long **e** sound you hear in *keep* and *green*.
- The letters **ea** can make the long **e** sound you hear in *bead*.
- The letters **ie** can make the long **e** sound you hear in *chief*.

Look at the pictures below. On the line, write the word that names each picture. Each picture name will have a long **e** sound.

_____   _____   _____

_____   _____   _____

Look at each picture below. Write the name of the picture next to it. Then, write each word from the box under the heading that has the same long **e** spelling.

treat	seed	reach	field	three	sea	collie	piece
sneeze	niece	beat	creek	chief	plead	speech	

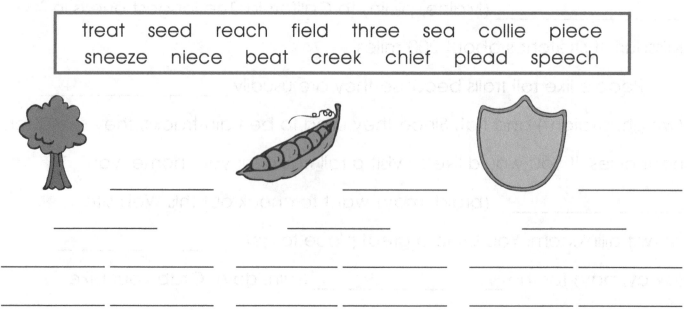

_____   _____   _____

_____   _____   _____

_____   _____   _____

_____   _____   _____

_____   _____   _____

Lesson 1.19 Vowel Sounds (ee, ea, ie)

Read the sentences and the pairs of letters that follow. Write the correct long **e** spelling on the line.

1. At the end of the w_____k, Ellie's class went on a field trip. (ee, ie)

2. They went to a p_____ch orchard out in the country. (ie, ea)

3. There were all kinds of f_____lds and farms near the orchard. (ee, ie)

4. Looking out the windows of the bus, the students saw dozens of wh_____t fields. (ea, ee)

5. They watched the stalks blow in the br_____ze. (ea, ee)

6. At the Gregors' farm, the peach tr_____s were full of fruit. (ie, ee)

7. Ellie and her friend, Omar, each picked thirt_____n peaches. (ee, ea)

8. The owner, Mrs. Gregor, said that a th_____f visits the orchard every night. (ea, ie)

9. Ellie and Omar laughed when they found out that it is a raccoon who st_____ls the fruit. (ie, ea)

10. When Mr. Zhou's class got back to school, they learned how to make a r_____l peach pie. (ea, ee)

11. They had to kn_____d the dough for only a few minutes. (ie, ea)

12. Mr. Zhou's class ate the warm pie with vanilla b_____n ice cr_____m. (ee, ea)

13. Everyone agr_____d it was the best field trip of the year. (ee, ie)

Lesson 1.20 Vowel Sounds (**ind**, **ild**, **igh**)

The vowel **i** can make a long sound when it is followed by the letters **nd**, **ld**, or **gh**.

f**ind**   beh**ind**   w**ild**   ch**ild**   s**igh**   n**igh**t

Read each meaning below. Choose a word from the box that matches the meaning. Write the word on the line.

blind   flashlight   wild   tight   thigh   behind   midnight   kind   child   mind

1. _____ the opposite of *loose*

2. _____ the part of the leg that is above the knee

3. _____ not tame; out of control

4. _____ 12 o'clock in the evening

5. _____ not able to see

6. _____ nice; sweet

7. _____ a young person

8. _____ the opposite of *in front of*

9. _____ something held in the hand that can help you see at night

10. _____ another word for *brain*

Lesson 1.20 Vowel Sounds (**ind**, **ild**, **igh**)

Read each sentence below. Complete the sentence with a word that rhymes with the word in parentheses ( ). The word you choose should make sense in the sentence.

1. My sister is the last _____ in a family of eight. (mild)

2. Austin said to make a _____ turn at the stop sign. (knight)

3. Uncle David has to _____ the old grandfather clock every few weeks. (mind)

4. The Simons had to _____ the house with candles when they lost power during the storm. (bright)

5. Did you follow the clues and _____ the treasure? (bind)

6. The books on the top shelf are too _____, and Parker cannot reach them. (sigh)

7. A new year begins at _____ on January 1st. (flashlight)

8. Three _____ bunnies live in Grandma's backyard and snack on the lettuce. (child)

Read the words below. One word in each set does not belong. Circle the word that has a different vowel sound than the others.

1. sigh	sing	right	5. rind	flip	fright
2. whip	grind	wild	6. chin	child	flight
3. mind	slight	sling	7. blind	bright	bit
4. tight	mild	trip	8. fight	hint	hind

Lesson 1.21 Vowel Sounds (**oa**, **ow**, **old**, **ost**)

> • The letters **oa** can make the **long o** sound you hear in c**oa**t and r**oa**m.
> • The letters **ow** can make the **long o** sound you hear in bl**ow** and r**ow**.
> • The vowel **o** can make a long sound when it is followed by the letters **ld** or **st**, as in c**old** and p**ost**.

Look at each picture. The letters beside the picture are scrambled. Unscramble them to form a word that matches the picture. Write the word on the line. Hint: Each word contains **oa**, **ow**, **old**, or **ost**.

dloc

oatts

wson

_____ _____ _____

Read the sentences below. Choose the word from the pair in parentheses ( ) that best completes the sentence. Write it on the line.

1. Ari's soccer team is going on the _____ (roast, road).

2. _____ (Coach, Goat) McKenna knows that her team has a good chance of winning the next game.

3. Ari hopes his team wins the _____ (gold, cold) medal at the end of the week.

4. Coach McKenna always tells the team that the _____ (most, show) important thing is that they have fun.

5. The first team they play is _____ (known, told) for being tough.

6. With only seconds left, Ari scores the winning _____ (goal, sold).

Lesson 1.21 Vowel Sounds (oa, ow, old, ost)

Read the clues below. Write the answers in the numbered spaces in the crossword puzzle. Each correct answer will have the long **o** sound spelled **oa**, **ow**, or **old**.

Across

2. the opposite of *young*
4. a slice of bread, lightly cooked
6. what you do to birthday candles
7. a green fuzz that grows on old food (rhymes with *bold*)
8. the past tense of the word *sell*

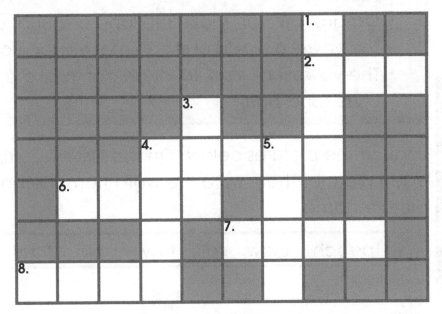

Down

1. what you wear when it's cold outside (rhymes with *goat*)
3. the opposite of *high*
4. an animal like a frog, except it has bumpy skin
5. white flakes that fall from the sky when it is cold

Read each word in bold. Then, circle the word beside it that has the same long vowel sound.

1. **slow**	sob	most	few
2. **fold**	foam	fast	from
3. **post**	row	rot	past
4. **croak**	creek	scold	cost
5. **flow**	coast	lost	cot
6. **coal**	cast	mop	mow

Review Vowel Sounds

- **Ai**, **ay**, and **ei** can all make the long **a** sound, as in *snail*, *may*, and *vein*.
- **Ee**, **ea**, and **ie** can all make the long **e** sound, as in *jeep*, *meat*, and *niece*.
- **Oa** and **ow** can make the long **o** sound, as in *coat* and *grown*.
- The vowel **o** plus **ld** or **st** can make a long **o** sound, as in *told* and *post*.
- The vowel **i** plus **nd**, **ld**, or **gh** can make a long **i** sound, as in *find*, *child*, and *sigh*.

Look at the pictures below. On the first line, write the word that names each picture. Then, write the word from the box that rhymes with each picture name.

| peach | glow | rail | tray | bold | float | weight | sigh | three |

Read the words below. One word in each set does not belong. Circle the word that has a different vowel sound than the others.

1. post   mold   sail   3. wild   rip   flight
2. bay   freeze   cheat   4. flap   fail   stray

Review Vowel Sounds

Read the paragraphs below. Each of the words in bold has a long vowel sound. Listen to the vowel sound and write each word in bold beside the correct heading.

The **sea** horse is a type of fish, but it probably looks different from any fish you've ever **seen**. Its head is shaped like a horse's head, which is how the sea horse got its name. Some people think the sea horse looks like a chess **piece** called a **knight**. Its body is covered with bony plates and small spines. The tip of its tail curls and can be used for clinging to plants.

Sea horses live in warm water. They are **weak** swimmers, so they don't usually go into **deep** water. Unlike most animals, the male is in charge of the eggs. He **keeps** them in his pouch until they are ready to hatch. Sea horses are also different from other fish because they swim **upright**.

Sea dragons are a member of the same family as sea horses. Sea dragons have long fins that flow around them. Some people think these fins look like **leaves**. The flowing fins help them hide in **fields** of seaweed that **sway** back and forth with the waves.

Project Sea Horse is one group that **feels** sea horses **need** to be protected. They are often caught in the **wild** by fishermen. Sometimes, they are used in making medicine. Sometimes, they are sold as pets. Project Sea Horse wants to **teach** the world about these interesting creatures. They hope the sea horses will **stay** around for a long time to come.

long **e** as in p**ea**: _____ _____ _____ _____

long **e** as in b**ee**p: _____ _____ _____ _____ _____

long **e** as in ch**ie**f: _____ _____

long **i** as in n**igh**t: _____ _____

long **i** as in ch**i**l**d**: _____

long **a** as in d**ay**: _____ _____

Lesson 1.22 Vowel Sounds (oo, ew)

- The letters **oo** can make the sound you hear in *boo*t and *bloo*m. They also make the sound you hear in *goo*d and *boo*k.
- The letters **ew** can make the sound you hear in *fl*ew and *n*ews.

Look at the pictures below. Write the word that names each picture on the first line. On the second line, write a rhyming word.

Read the paragraphs below. Circle the word from each pair that best completes the sentences.

You may not know who A. A. Milne is, but there is a (wood, good) chance you have read some of his (books, scoops). A (few, chew) of them have even been made into (spools, cartoons). Milne wrote the Winnie the (Pooh, Hood) books that children around the world know and love. He wrote the stories for his young son, Christopher. The characters in the books are based on Christopher's toys. Pooh was one of Christopher's stuffed bears. Kanga was a mother (moose, kangaroo), and Roo was her baby. Another character was a (moon, gloomy) donkey named *Eeyore*.

In most of the stories, Christopher Robin and his (goose, crew) of animal friends have adventures. Of course, the real Christopher Robin (few, grew) up over time. The Pooh stories end when the human boy goes to (school, mood) and becomes (new, too) old to play with his stuffed friends all day. No one (knew, noon) what a big hit A. A. Milne's nursery stories would be.

Lesson 1.22 Vowel Sounds (oo, ew)

Circle the two words in each set that have the same vowel sound.

1. chew   stew   chop   5. hoot   dew   hot

2. zoo   brown   drool   6. gloom   loop   crook

3. fleck   spoon   flew   7. foot   noon   hood

4. stood   brook   new   8. book   goose   snooze

Read the paragraphs below. Pay careful attention to the sentences in bold. Circle the words in those sentences that have the **oo** or **ew** spelling.

The harvest moon can be seen around September 23 every year. It appears during the fall equinox. An equinox is the time of year when day and night are the same length.

The harvest moon looks bigger than other full moons. This is because it hangs low in the sky. **The moon is always the same size, but it just seems to loom bigger during the harvest moon.** It also rises not long after sunset.

The harvest moon got its name from farmers. **It took them a long time to harvest crops in the fall. It was good for the farmers to have the extra light. They knew they would have more time to harvest their crops, because the big, yellow moon lit up the fields.**

Did you know that the full moons of other months have names too? Naming moons is not a new idea. It is one way people kept track of time before today's calendars. **Some other moon names are Corn Moon, Wolf Moon, Hunter's Moon, Snow Moon, and Flower Moon.** Can you guess how they got their names?

Lesson 1.23 Vowel Sounds (**au**, **aw**)

- The letters **au** can make the sound you hear in s**au**ce and c**au**ght.
- The letters **aw** can make the sound you hear in dr**aw** and l**aw**n.

Read each word in bold. Circle the word beside it that has the same vowel sound.

1. **claw**   bawl   cast   bowl
2. **taught** tank   law   wind
3. **fault**   caught   fat   fume
4. **jaw**   jail   cow   dawn

5. **yawn**   slaw   sail   wow
6. **straw**   hay   launch   ant
7. **auto**   tame   gnaw   runt
8. **shawl**   shop   tan   raw

Read each clue below. On the line, write the word from the box that matches the clue.

| August straw yawn author paw fawn crawl auto saw lawn |

1. _____ the way babies move around

2. _____ the green grassy area around a house

3. _____ another word for *writer*

4. _____ something you do when you feel sleepy

5. _____ the month that comes between July and September

6. _____ an animal's foot

7. _____ another name for *car*

8. _____ a sharp tool used for cutting wood

9. _____ a young deer

10. _____ a long, skinny tube that you put in a glass and drink from

NAME _____

Lesson 1.23 Vowel Sounds (**au, aw**)

Look at the pictures below. Fill in the blanks to complete each picture name.

cl____ ____ ____   ____ ____tumn   h____ ____k

cr____ ____l   y____ ____n   l____ ____ndry

Read each sentence and the set of words that follows it. Choose the word that best completes the sentence and write it on the line.

1. The scientists will _____ the rocket at 2:15.

     sauce   jaw   launch

2. What is your favorite book, and who is the _____?

     author   auto   shawl

3. Daniel's grandma _____ him how to count to ten in Spanish.

     awful   taught   fawn

4. We can't ride our bikes _____ it's raining.

     because   caution   fault

5. Habib put together a _____ puzzle with 150 pieces.

     awful   draw   jigsaw

6. Callie's favorite dish at the diner is _____ and pancakes.

     slaw   sausage   drawn

Lesson 1.24 Vowel Sounds (oi, oy)

> • The letters **oi** make the sound you hear in *boil* and *spoil*.
> • The letters **oy** make the sound you hear in *boy* and *joy*.

Read each clue below. Write **oi** or **oy** on the line to form a word that matches the clue.

1. part of the king and queen's family   r____ ____al

2. things kids like to play with   t____ ____s

3. a long trip or journey   v____ ____age

4. the opposite of *girl*   b____ ____

5. another word for *dirt*   s____ ____l

6. liquid that is so hot it begins to bubble   b____ ____l

Underline the words in the sentences below that have the /oi/ sound spelled **oi** or **oy**. The number in parentheses ( ) will tell you how many words you should find in each sentence.

1. Roy and Troy McCoy are twin cowboys. (4)

2. Sometimes, they annoy each other, but the brothers are always loyal. (2)

3. One day, Roy joined his brother on a voyage across the prairie. (3)

4. Troy, who enjoys using a lasso, coiled some rope on his saddle. (3)

5. "Look, Troy," said Roy, pointing at a herd of wild buffalo. "An entire herd of buffalo can make a lot of noise!" (4)

6. After a long day on the prairie, the McCoy brothers ate some burgers they broiled in a fire pit. (2)

7. "There is nothing as good as boiled corn and sirloin cooked in foil over a campfire," agreed the cowboys. (4)

Lesson 1.24 Vowel Sounds (oi, oy)

Draw a line from each word in bold to a rhyming word beside it.

1. oil	royal		**4. soy**	soil
	enjoy			choice
	ballpoint			boy
2. coin	noise		**5. joint**	point
	broiler			moist
	join			foil
3. loyal	joy		**6. choice**	poison
	spoil			voice
	avoid			tinfoil

Underline the word that best completes each sentence below.

1. Molly likes the salty taste of (soy, toy) sauce on her food when she visits China Garden Restaurant.
2. Ravi likes to collect (foil, coins) from different countries around the world.
3. Dogs are known for being (loyal, annoy) to their masters.
4. Sumiko has a beautiful (oyster, voice), so she will sing in the school play.
5. There was so much (soil, noise) at the birthday party, Ms. Silva didn't hear the phone ring.
6. Elliot hoped the storm wouldn't (spoil, joyful) his plan to go on a picnic.
7. The (avoid, point) on this pencil isn't sharp at all.
8. Chris (joined, boiled) the soccer club and the theater club at his new school.

Lesson 1.25 Vowel Sounds (ou, ow)

> • The letters **ou** make the sound you hear in *pr**ou**d* and *sh**ou**t*.
> • The letters **ow** make the sound you hear in *n**ow*** and *t**ow**n*.

Look at each picture below. On the line, write the word that names the picture. Then, circle the word that rhymes with the picture name.

_____   _____   _____

proud   now   cod   count   brown   old   hunt   how   blouse

Read the sentences below. Choose the word from the pair in parentheses ( ) that best completes each sentence. Write it on the line.

1. Charlie _____ is a popular character from the comic strip "Peanuts." (Brown, Flour)

2. The author of the comic, Charles Schultz, was _____ of the funny characters he created. (out loud, proud)

3. Charlie has terrible luck and seems to walk through life with a _____ hanging above his head. (count, cloud)

4. Charlie Brown has a clever _____ named *Snoopy*. (plow, hound)

5. Snoopy is known for sleeping on top of his _____. (doghouse, crown)

6. Charlie tries to kick the football. Lucy holds for him, but he usually ends up on the _____. (scout, ground)

Lesson 1.25 Vowel Sounds (**ou**, **ow**)

Read the clues below. Underline the word that matches each clue.

1. I am a word that describes someone who is grumpy or crabby.

    couch   grouch   sprout

2. I am a sound that wolves make. Dogs can make this sound, too. What am I?

    howl   mouse   ounce

3. I am a white or light brown powder used in baking. What am I?

    down   ground   flour

4. I am the face people make when they are sad. What am I?

    frown   sound   spout

5. I am a measurement of weight. What am I?

    out   pound   loud

6. I am the opposite of sweet. I am the flavor of lemons. What am I?

    town   sour   growl

7. I am what farmers must do to their fields before they plant. What am I?

    pout   bounce   plow

Read the words below. Circle the word that has the same vowel sound as the word in bold.

1. now	trout	newt	sold
2. spout	trust	scowl	mumps
3. sound	sun	rude	pouch
4. brow	gown	broil	gold
5. crouch	must	crunch	hour
6. south	booth	town	such
7. cow	rob	cute	growl

Review More Vowel Sounds

> • The letters **oo** and **ew** can make the sound you hear in g**oo**se and
> ch**ew**. The letters **oo** can also make the sound you hear in c**oo**k.
> • The letters **au** and **aw** can make the sound you hear in c**au**ght
> and s**aw**.
> • The letters **oi** and **oy** can make the sound you hear in c**oi**n and t**oy**.
> • The letters **ou** and **ow** can make the sound you hear in p**ou**nce
> and gr**ow**l.

Read the clues in column 1. Draw a line to match each clue to its correct "hink pink" in column 2.

1. a cozy place for reading   mouse house

2. a dog that eats too much   stew crew

3. a fun place to swim   loose goose

4. a group of people who make soup   round hound

5. the nose of a fish   book nook

6. a trusty queen   trout snout

7. a home for a rodent   cool pool

8. a bird that got away   loyal royal

Read each sentence below. Circle the word that has the same vowel sound as the word in parentheses ( ).

1. Emily put on her straw hat and began picking vegetables. (sauce)

2. Marcus's dad gave him several coins for his collection. (joy)

3. The tiny gray kittens pounce on the ball of string. (wow)

4. The geese flew over Desiree's house as they headed south for the winter. (broom)

5. Tomás stood in front of the audience and bowed. (cook)

Review More Vowel Sounds

Write the word that names each picture below. Then, write the words from the box under the heading with the same vowel sound.

lawn	bounce	flew	caught	gown	boot
brew	prowl	draw	sauce	zoo	hour

_____   _____   _____

_____   _____   _____

_____   _____   _____

_____   _____   _____

Read the paragraphs below. Circle the word from each pair in parentheses ( ) that best completes the sentence.

A raptor is a bird, like a (hawk, claw) or an eagle, that preys on other animals. The Carolina Raptor Center is a safe place for these birds when they have been hurt. The people at the center rescue raptors they have (found, proud) and help them heal. Many of the birds they've (sound, caught) are released into the wild once they feel better. Birds that can no longer survive in the wild (avoid, join) the family. There, they will always have a (good, goose) home and (wood, food) to eat.

People can (enjoy, saw) the nature trails and see the birds in large, airy mesh cages. Some birds travel to (blooms, schools) so that children can learn about their interesting habits. An (owl, auto) named *Omar* likes being around people so much, he gets depressed (without, now) them!

Lesson 1.26 The Sounds of **y**

- At the beginning of a word, the letter **y** can make the sound you hear in **y**ellow and **y**es.
- The letter **y** can make the long **i** sound, as in sp**y** and cr**y**.
- It can also make the long **e** sound, as in bell**y** and rust**y**.

Read each set of words below. Write **y**, *long i*, or *long e* on the line to show what sound the letter **y** makes in all the words in the set.

1. _____   tiny   quickly   story

2. _____   fly   dry   my

3. _____   sixty   chilly   candy

4. _____   yet   yak   yolk

5. _____   cry   sky   spy

6. _____   carry   windy   messy

7. _____   yourself   yogurt   yank

Read the clues below. On the line, write the word that matches each clue. Make sure that the word you choose has the correct sound of **y**.

1. I am the number that comes after thirty-nine. (long **e**) _____

2. I am the opposite of *wet*. (long **i**) _____

3. People eat me on sandwiches with peanut butter. (long **e**) _____

4. I am the opposite of *old*. (**y**) _____

5. I am a coin worth one cent. (long **e**) _____

6. I am the color of lemons and the sun. (**y**) _____

Lesson 1.26 The Sounds of y

Read the paragraphs below. Each of the words in bold contains the letter **y**. Listen to the sound the **y** makes. Write each word in bold under the correct heading. An example has been added below each heading to help you.

Tyler got his first **yo-yo** when he was **only** four **years** old. It was a favor at a birthday **party**. Tyler liked the way the **shiny** red disks sparkled in the sun. When he picked it up, his hands knew just what to do.

Five years later, Tyler is one of the best yo-yo players in the **city**. Just ask him to **try** a new trick, and watch the yo-yo **fly** into the air. Tyler can make all kinds of **tricky** moves look **easy**. He has videos of some of the most famous young yo-yo players in the **country**. When they **yank** the string with a flick of the wrist, the yo-yo goes **exactly** where they want it.

Tyler hasn't gone to any competitions **yet**, but **lately** he has spent a lot of time practicing. He can do tricks like "hop the fence," "walk the dog," "rock the **baby**," and "over the falls." He might be **young**, but Tyler has all the makings of a true yo-yo champ.

long **i**	long **e**		**y**
by	*thirsty*		*yard*
_____	_____	_____	_____
_____	_____	_____	_____
_____	_____	_____	_____
	_____	_____	_____
	_____	_____	

Lesson 1.27 R-Controlled Vowels (er, ir, ur)

When the letter **r** comes after a vowel, it can change the sound of the vowel. The letters **er**, **ir**, and **ur** can all make the same sound, as in p**er**ch, f**ir**m, and s**ur**f.

Look at the pictures below. Write the name of each picture on the line. Then, circle the pair of letters that make the /ur/ sound.

_____   _____   _____

_____   _____   _____

Read each word. Write the letter of its definition on the line.

1. _____ mother

2. _____ circus

3. _____ birthday

4. _____ purple

5. _____ verb

6. _____ purr

7. _____ winter

8. _____ germ

9. _____ fur

10. _____ stir

a. the day of the year a person was born

b. a part of speech that shows action

c. a cold, snowy season

d. something very tiny that can make you sick

e. a woman who has children

f. the color that is a mix of red and blue

g. the hair that covers an animal's body

h. to mix or blend

i. a show with clowns, animals, and the trapeze

j. a noise cats make when they are happy

Lesson 1.27 R-Controlled Vowels (er, ir, ur)

Read the sentences below. Write **ir**, **er**, or **ur** to complete the words. The words you form should make sense in the sentences.

1. The park near my house is quiet in wint_____.

2. The trees are bare, so I can see dozens of b_____ds p_____ched in the branches.

3. The wat_____ in the riv_____ doesn't freeze because it moves so quickly.

4. I love watching deer b_____st through the woods with their white tails bouncing along behind them.

5. Last Th_____sday, I saw a moth_____ deer and her baby come to the river to drink.

6. I've even seen a couple of t_____keys walking along the edge of a field.

7. When snowflakes start to tw_____l and wh_____l through the air, I know it's time to head for home.

8. Oth_____ people might prefer warm weath_____, but there's nothing like winter at the park for me.

Underline the letters that make the /ur/ sound in each word in bold below. Then, circle the word beside it that has the same sound.

1. **herd**	shirt	head	red
2. **perk**	peck	under	itch
3. **purse**	must	girl	punch
4. **birthday**	pig	wrist	fern
5. **curve**	chirp	cut	rug
6. **dirty**	mist	nest	person

Lesson 1.28 R-Controlled Vowels (ar, or)

When the letter **r** comes after a vowel, it can change the sound of the vowel.
- The letters **ar** can make the sound you hear in p**ar**ty and ch**ar**m.
- The letters **or** can make the sound you hear in f**or**k and sp**or**t.

On the first line, write the word that names each picture below. Then, write the words from the box under the heading with the same vowel sound.

| thorn | arch | cart | sport | scar | tart | porch | cord |

_____   _____

_____   _____

_____   _____

_____   _____

Read the definitions below. On the line, write the word from the box that matches each definition.

| snore | garden | fork | yarn | large | north |

1. the opposite of *small* _____

2. an area where people grow flowers and plants _____

3. a piece of silverware used for spearing food _____

4. a type of thick thread or string used for knitting _____

5. a noise that some people make when they sleep _____

6. the opposite of *south* _____

Lesson 1.28 R-Controlled Vowels (ar, or)

Read the paragraphs below. Underline the word from each pair in parentheses ( ) that best completes the sentences.

Have you ever gone to a (farmers', marchers') market? They can be a great place to visit on a Saturday (porch, morning). Some are located near (cars, farms) in the country. Others are right in the middle of cities. One reason people enjoy shopping at (markets, scarves) instead of (sports, stores) is that everything they buy is so fresh. Sometimes, it is also less expensive. If you buy a tomato that had (far, for) to travel before it reached your grocery store, you will be (charged, formed) more (fort, for) it.

At a farmers' market, you can buy things that are in season and grown nearby. How about some (large, sharp), ripe peaches, crisp cucumbers, or sweet (cork, corn)? Many markets sell (more, sort) than just fruits and vegetables. For example, you may be able to buy organic meat, like (horn, pork) or chicken. *Organic* means that the animals ate only natural foods. (Organic, Morning) vegetables are not sprayed with chemicals. Other markets have (arts, marks) and crafts or baked goods for sale.

Do you have a (garden, harp) at home? If you live in a city, there may be a community garden nearby. If you grow more vegetables or flowers than you can use, think about taking your extras to a farmers' market. All you need is a (march, cart) or a stand. Your business may (yarn, start) out small and grow (larger, shorter) every week!

Review The Sounds of **y** and **r**-Controlled Vowels

Read the clues below. Circle the word that matches each clue.

1. I am a piece of clothing worn around the neck in cold weather. What am I?

    skirt scarf sport

2. I am a person who doesn't like to be seen. Sometimes, I go undercover and secretly watch people. What am I?

    happy spy shy

3. I am the opposite of the word *before*. What am I?

    under verb after

4. I am an animal that people ride. I make the sound *neigh*. You can find me on a farm. What am I?

    horse bird river

5. I am the group of people you are related to. What am I?

    family happy quickly

6. I am like a sweet potato. I can be baked or mashed. What am I?

    yacht yellow yam

7. I am usually made of glass. I can be used for storing things, like jam or sauce. What am I?

    jar stork porch

8. I am something you might write to a friend. I usually begin with the word *dear*.

    term other letter

9. I am the yellow part of an egg. What am I?

    sunny yolk yogurt

10. I am a reptile. I carry my shell on my back for protection. What am I?

    germ fern turtle

Review The Sounds of **y** and **r**-Controlled Vowels

Draw a line from each word in bold to the word beside it that has the same **r**-controlled vowel sound.

1. **third**
verse
shore
think

2. **marsh**
dash
star
clerk

3. **curb**
cut
short
shirt

4. **torn**
mark
cork
tug

5. **chore**
torch
shop
jar

6. **curl**
mutt
chart
germ

7. **spark**
fort
bag
dart

8. **core**
cost
sword
trust

Read the sentences below. Circle words that contain the letter **y**. On the line, write the sound of **y** you hear (**y**, long **i**, or long **e**) in the words you circled.

1. After I dry this pan, I'm going to fry the fish I caught with my dad. _____

2. The baby bunny was lucky to find crisp lettuce in the pretty garden. _____

3. Yesterday, Yoko yelled when she got stung by a yellow jacket. _____

4. Aaron will fly his kite high in the sky at the park. _____

Lesson 2.1 Base Words and Endings (-ed, -ing)

A **base word** is a word without any endings added to it.

- If a base word has a short vowel sound and ends in a consonant, double the consonant before adding **ed** or **ing**.

    rub   rub**bed**   rub**bing**

- If a base word ends with **e**, drop the **e** before adding **ed** or **ing**.

    taste   tast**ed**   tast**ing**

- If a base word ends with **y**, change the **y** to **i** before adding **ed**. Do not change the **y** before adding **ing**.

    cry   cr**ied**   cr**ying**

Fill in the blanks in the chart below.

Base Word	Add ed	Add ing
	chopped	
		hiking
bloom		
plan		
		spying
hope		
		humming
carry		
	suggested	
		clapping
try		
		acting
hug		

Lesson 2.1 Base Words and Endings (-**ed**, -**ing**)

Read the paragraphs below. Underline the word from the pair in parentheses ( ) that correctly completes each sentence.

Ellis Island is (located, locateed) in New York Harbor. Immigrants, or people (moveing, moving) to the United States from other countries, usually passed through Ellis Island. They had to be (interviewed, interviewd) before they were (allowing, allowed) to enter the country. They also had to be (examined, examineed) by a doctor to make sure they were healthy. If relatives of yours came to America from Europe during the early 1900s, they probably (passed, passing) through Ellis Island.

People who were (traveled, traveling) by boat could see the Statue of Liberty as they made their way into New York Harbor. Some people (cried, cryed) when they first saw it. Ellis Island and the famous statue were both signs to immigrants that their new life was (started, starting). Today, there is a museum on Ellis Island. If you are interested in (seing, seeing) whether any relatives of yours (stopped, stoped) at Ellis Island, you can try checking the passenger list at www.ellisisland.org.

Read the sentences below. Write the base word for each word in bold.

1. Elizabeth made a family tree when her class
   studied Ellis Island.   _____

2. After **quizzing** her mom, she did some research
   on the Internet.   _____

3. Elizabeth learned that her great-grandparents
   had **lived** in Ireland.   _____

4. They were **married** when they were only
   17 years old.   _____

Lesson 2.2   Base Word Endings (-s, -es)

New words can be formed by adding **s** or **es** to base words.
- Just add **s** to the end of many action words to change their form.
  Tim and Maya *smile*.   Maya *smile**s***.
- If an action word ends with **y**, change the **y** to **i** and add **es**.
  Mom and Dad *worry*. Mom *worr**ies***.
- If an action word ends with **s**, **sh**, **ch**, **x**, or **z**, add **es**.
  They *search*.   Mr. Fitz *search**es***.

Read the sentences below. On the line, write the correct form of the base words in bold.

1. The excited beagles **bark**.   The excited beagle

   _____.

2. We **coax** the kittens to eat.   Lee _____ the kittens to eat.

3. Gabby and Eric **study** for the quiz.   Gabby _____ for the quiz.

4. The teachers **ring** the bell.   Ms. Spitzer _____ the bell.

5. Cody and his brother **latch** the gate.   Cody _____ the gate.

6. Grandma and Grandpa **kiss** the babies.   Grandma _____ the babies.

7. We **empty** the bucket of water.   Lauren _____ the bucket of water.

8. The boys **wax** the car.   Ethan _____ the car.

Lesson 2.2 Base Word Endings (-**s**, -**es**)

Read the sentences below. Circle the words that best complete the sentences.

1. Katie (tosses, toss's) the red squeaky toy across the backyard.

2. Buster (rushs, rushes) after it at full speed.

3. He (trys, tries) to stop and almost (crashes, crashs) into the fence.

4. "Slow down, Buster," (calls, calles) Katie, as she (watchs, watches) him skid.

5. Buster (wags, waggs) his tail and happily (bringes, brings) the squeaky toy back to his friend.

6. Katie (kiss's, kisses) Buster on his wet nose and (givs, gives) him a treat.

7. Buster (hurrys, hurries) to the far corner of the backyard where he (buries, burys) it.

Read each word below. On the line, write the base word.

1. mixes _____   7. claps _____

2. fries _____   8. cries _____

3. talks _____   9. hisses _____

4. crunches _____   10. dances _____

5. marries _____   11. washes _____

6. brushes _____   12. bakes _____

Lesson 2.3 Comparative Endings (-**er**, -**est**)

> • The endings -**er** and -**est** can be added to base words to make a comparison.
>
>   Add **er** to mean *more*.   loud**er** = more loud
>   Add **est** to mean *most*.   loud**est** = most loud
>
> • For words that end in **e**, drop the **e** and add **er** or **est**.
>   wise   wis**er**   wis**est**
>
> • For words that end in a consonant and **y**, change the **y** to **i** before adding **er** or **est**.
>   funny   funn**ier**   funn**iest**
>
> • For words that have a short vowel sound and end in a consonant, double the consonant before adding **er** or **est**.
>   big   big**ger**   big**gest**

Read the sentences below. On the line, write the comparative form of the words in parentheses ( ).

1. The _____ place in the world that people live is Dallol, Ethiopia. It can be 145 degrees in the sun! (most hot)

2. Aswan, Egypt, is the _____ place in the world, with only $\frac{2}{100}$ of an inch of rain each year. (most dry)

3. Mt. Waialeale, Hawaii, is the _____ place in the United States. It gets about 460 inches of rain per year. (most wet)

4. Mt. Waialeale is _____ than Mt. Washington, New Hampshire. (more wet)

5. It is _____ in Yuma, Arizona, than in Las Vegas, Nevada. (more sunny)

6. Resolute, Canada, is one of the _____ places people live. Only about 200 people stay there all year long. (most cold)

Lesson 2.3 Comparative Endings (-**er**, -**est**)

Fill in the blanks with the correct form of the comparative word.

Base Word	Add er	Add est
	safer	
thin		
sweet		sweetest
		warmest
strange		
busy		

Read the sentences below. Underline the word in each pair that correctly completes the sentence.

1. The Boxley family has six cats. Brady is the (friendliest, friendlier).
2. Besty is (quietest, quieter) than Blossom and Bridget.
3. Benjamin is the (largeest, largest) cat.
4. Blaze is (gentler, gentlest) than his brothers and sisters.
5. Blossom has bright orange fur and is definitely the (fluffyest, fluffiest) cat.
6. Bridget is a picky eater, so she is (thinner, thiner) than the others.
7. Mrs. Boxley thinks Blaze is (smarter, smartest) than Brady and Benjamin.

Phonics Connection

Write beginning **l** blend and **r** blend words from the sentences above.

l blend: _____ _____ _____

r blend: _____ _____ _____

_____ _____ _____

Review Base Words and Endings

Here are some reminders about adding endings to base words.
- If a base word ends with **e**, drop the **e** before adding the endings **-ed**, **-ing**, **-er**, or **-est**.   skate skat**ed** skat**ing**
- For words that have a short vowel sound and end in a consonant, double the consonant before adding the endings **-ed**, **-ing**, **-er**, or **-est**.   hot hot**ter** hot**test**
- For words that end in a consonant and **y**, change the **y** to **i** before adding the endings **-ed**, **-es**, **-er**, or **-est**. (Do not change the **y** before adding **ing**.)   cry cr**ied** cr**ies** cr**ying**
- If a word ends with **s**, **sh**, **ch**, **x**, or **z**, add **es**.   rush rush**es**
- When making a comparison, add **er** to mean *more*. Add **est** to mean *most*.   soft**er** = more soft   soft**est** = most soft

Fill in the blanks to complete the chart below.

Base Word	Add s or es	Add ed	Add ing
watch			
		tasted	
	finishes		
skip			
			missing
relax			
		laughed	
	tries		
			jumping
explore			
		fussed	
	drips		
			worrying

Review Base Words and Endings

Solve each problem below. Be sure to remember the rules for adding endings. Then, write a sentence using your answer.

1. small + er = _____

   _____

2. strange + est = _____

   _____

3. funny + est = _____

   _____

4. big + est = _____

   _____

Read the paragraphs below. Underline the word from the pair in parentheses ( ) that correctly completes each sentence.

Clara Barton always (likd, liked) helping others. When the Civil War began, she made bandages for the war effort. Clara wanted to make a (bigger, biger) difference, though. She began (worked, working) near the front lines. She was one of the (gentlest, gentler) volunteers there. Clara was (braver, bravest) than many people who were close to the battlefront. Even when she was in danger, she never thought of (quiting, quitting).

After spending time in Europe, Clara saw the good work that the Red Cross was doing. By (talked, talking) to important people and (makeing, making) speeches, Clara got some attention. In 1881, Clara Barton (founded, foundes) the American Red Cross. She would be (pleasing, pleased) to know that the group she organized still (touches, touchs) many lives today.

Lesson 2.4   Plurals

The word **plural** means *more than one*.
- To make most words plural, just add **s**.   book books   bell bells
- If a noun ends in **sh, ch, s,** or **x**, add **es**.   fox fox**es**   bush bush**es**
- If a noun ends with a consonant and **y**, drop the **y** and add **ies**.
  fly fl**ies**   city cit**ies**
- For some words that end in **f** or **fe**, change the **f** or **fe** to **v** and
  add **es**.   wolf wol**ves**   loaf loa**ves**

Look at the pictures below. On the first line, write the word that names each picture. On the second line, write the plural form of the word.

Read the sentences below. On the line, write the correct plural form of the word in parentheses ( ).

1. The park was filled with the _____ of Little League players. (family)

2. Each of the _____ gave their teams a few last words of advice. (coach)

3. Alex, the Cougars' pitcher, wound up and nodded at his _____ (teammate)

4. Clare hit the ball and ran two _____ before she was tagged out. (base)

Lesson 2.4 Plurals

Write the word from the box that matches each clue below. Then, find the plural form of each word in the puzzle. Circle the words you find.

| spoon | class | leaf | diary | party | thief | peach | pony | dolphin |

1. _____ an event where people get together to celebrate

2. _____ someone who steals things

3. _____ a piece of silverware used for eating soup

4. _____ a small horse

5. _____ a sweet, pale-orange summer fruit

6. _____ a friendly gray mammal that lives in the ocean

7. _____
a group of children who go to the same school and have the same teacher

8. _____
a book in which people record the things that happen to them

9. _____
the small, flat green part of a plant or tree

t	h	i	e	v	e	s	j	x	s
h	e	p	e	a	c	h	e	s	a
n	d	o	l	p	h	i	n	s	u
r	i	n	e	t	h	x	c	q	a
c	a	i	g	a	t	o	l	r	k
b	r	e	u	d	n	y	a	a	s
o	i	s	p	o	o	n	s	t	t
f	e	k	t	f	p	j	s	o	b
y	s	r	l	e	a	v	e	s	v
w	p	a	r	t	i	e	s	d	l

Lesson 2.5 Irregular Plurals

Some plural words are **irregular**. They do not follow the rules, so you must memorize their plural forms.

child children   foot feet   mouse mice   goose geese
woman women   man men   ox oxen   die dice

The singular and plural forms of some words are the same.
deer   fish   moose   sheep   trout   series   species

Read each word below. Choose the correct plural form from the words beside it and circle it.

1. **child**   childs   children   childes

2. **sheep**   sheep   sheeps   sheepes

3. **woman**   womans   womens   women

4. **moose**   meese   moose   mooses

5. **goose**   gooses   geeses   geese

Use the pictures to help you fill in the blanks in the math problems below.

1. one [sheep] + one [sheep] = two _____

2. one [goose] + two _____ = three geese

3. one [mouse] + one _____ = two _____

4. three [people] – one man = two _____

Lesson 2.5 Irregular Plurals

Complete each sentence below with a word from the box. On the line at the end of the sentence, write **S** if the singular form of the word is used. Write **P** if the plural form is used.

| series   oxen   feet   moose   die   trout   children |

1. The large, brown _____ stood at the edge of the forest

   and shook his antlers. _____

2. Last weekend, Grandpa and I caught three _____ in the

   mountain stream. _____

3. How many _____ will be going on the field trip? _____

4. If your _____ are cold, put on a thicker pair of socks. _____

5. Is that book part of your favorite _____? _____

6. Roll the _____ and move your piece clockwise around

   the game board. _____

Read each pair of sentences below. Circle the letter of the sentence in which the word in bold is used correctly.

1. **a.** Three of the **mans** take the subway to work.

   b. Three of the **men** take the subway to work.

2. **a.** Maureen named the **mice** *Harold* and *Cupcake*.

   b. Maureen named the **mouses** *Harold* and *Cupcake*.

3. **a.** You can see 19 **species** of frogs at the Woodlake Nature Center.

   b. You can see 19 **specieses** of frogs at the Woodlake Nature Center.

4. **a.** What types of **fishes** did you see at the aquarium?

   b. What types of **fish** did you see at the aquarium?

Lesson 2.6 Possessives

A **possessive** is a word that shows ownership. Adding an apostrophe
(') plus **s** to a word makes it possessive.

Dante**'s** jacket   Mr. Fargo**'s** mail   the shirt**'s** collar

Even when a singular word ends in **s**, add **'s** to form the possessive.
the boss**'s** desk   Tess**'s** backpack   Dr. Jones**'s** office

Read each phrase below. On the line, write the possessive form.

1. the homework of Will _____

2. the tail of the squirrel _____

3. the keyboard of the computer _____

4. the gym of the school _____

5. the eyes of Charles _____

6. the actors of the movie _____

7. the books of the library _____

8. the smile of Malika _____

9. the colors of the dress _____

Read the sentences below. If the word in bold is plural, write **PL** on the line.
If it is possessive, write **PO**.

1. _____ The trapeze **artists** flew through the air.

2. _____ The **lion's** roar shook the seats in the circus tent.

3. _____ The elephants ate **peanuts** from their trainer's hand.

4. _____ The **clown's** nose was round and red.

5. _____ The **ringmaster's** routine made the fans laugh.

Lesson 2.6   Possessives

> Add an apostrophe (') to the end of a plural word to form a **plural possessive**.
>
>   the girls' books   the monkeys' food   the teachers' classrooms
>
> If a plural word does not end in **s**, add an apostrophe plus **s** ('**s**).
>   the children**'s** lunch   the people**'s** votes   the men**'s** ideas

Read each phrase below. On the line, write the plural possessive.

1. the tents of the campers_____

2. the sleeping bags of the boys_____

3. the flames of the campfires_____

4. the chirping of the crickets_____

5. the singing of the children_____

6. the zippers of the backpacks_____

7. the beams of the flashlights_____

8. the smells of the food_____

Phonics Connection

In the exercise above, five words contain digraphs. Write the words on the lines below and circle the digraphs.

_____   _____   _____

_____   _____

Lesson 2.6 Possessives

Read each phrase below. If it is plural, write **PL** on the line. If it is singular possessive, write **SP**. If it is plural possessive, write **PP**.

1. _____ Jack's canary

2. _____ the cats' water bowl

3. _____ the baby gerbils

4. _____ Akiko's guinea pig

5. _____ the Stosaks' turtles

6. _____ the lizards' cage

7. _____ the barking sheepdogs

8. _____ the rabbit's foot

Read the sentences below. Circle the letter of the word that correctly completes each sentence.

1. Eliza is watching the _____ pets while they are out of town.

   a. Howells'

   b. Howells's

2. _____ job is to feed the goldfish and the hamsters, Harriet and Hank.

   a. Elizas

   b. Eliza's

3. The _____ cage is filled with cedar chips.

   a. hamster's

   b. hamsters

4. Eliza drops flakes of food into the _____ tank.

   a. goldfish's

   b. goldfishes's

Phonics Connection

In the first exercise above, three words begin with hard **c**. One word begins with hard **g** and one begins with soft **g**. List the words below.

Hard c: _____ _____ _____

Hard g: _____

Soft g: _____

Lesson 2.6 Possessives

Rewrite each sentence, replacing the words in bold with a possessive.

1. The **teacher of the sisters** is Mrs. Huong.

   _____

2. The **schedule for the bus** is posted on the bulletin board.

   _____

3. The lyrics are on the inside of **the case of the CD**.

   _____

4. **A friend of Antoine** will be here at noon.

   _____

5. The **pieces of the game** are still inside the box.

   _____

6. The **wings of the butterflies** seem to shimmer in the sunlight.

   _____

7. Be careful not to let go of **the strings of the balloons**.

   _____

8. The **frame of the painting** is cracked.

   _____

9. The **jackets of the skaters** were warm and cozy.

   _____

10. The **ring of the alarm clock** is loud and shrill.

   _____

Review Plurals and Possessives

Fill in the blanks to complete the chart below. The first row is done for you.

Singular	Plural	Singular Possessive	Plural Possessive
book	books	book's	books'
woman			women's
	wolves	wolf's	
egg			eggs'
library		library's	
sheep		sheep's	
	mice		mice's
dish			dishes'
		city's	cities'

On the first line, write the plural form of each word. On the second line, write a phrase using the plural possessive form.

Example: bike   bikes _____   bikes' tires _____

1. school   _____   _____

2. bus   _____   _____

3. leaf   _____   _____

4. beach   _____   _____

5. country   _____   _____

6. computer   _____   _____

7. story   _____   _____

8. fox   _____   _____

Review Plurals and Possessives

Read the paragraph below. If the word in bold is plural, write **PL** on the line. If it is singular possessive, write **SP**. If it is plural possessive, write **PP**.

The highest waterfalls _____ in North America are in California's _____ Yosemite National Park. The falls _____ are 2,425 feet tall. That is about 13 times as tall as Niagara Falls. Yosemite is near the Sierra Nevada Mountains. In the spring, the mountains' _____ snow begins to melt. The melted snow fills the rivers _____ and feeds the waterfalls. By the end of summer, most of the park's _____ falls are pretty dry.

Read the sentences below. Underline the word that correctly completes each sentence.

1. John (Muir's, Muirs') dream was to preserve Yosemite as a national park.
2. Grizzly bears used to live in Yosemite, but no (grizzlys, grizzlies) are found there today.
3. Native American (tribes', tribes) lived in the area before explorers arrived.
4. The sequoia (trees', trees) trunks reach hundreds of feet into the air.
5. There are more than 250 (species, specieses) of animals at Yosemite.
6. (Grasses, Grass') in the meadows provide food for many animals.
7. (Hikeres, Hikers) can enjoy more than 800 miles of trails.
8. Thousands of (familys, families) visit the park every year.
9. It is not unusual to see (deers, deer), skunks, beavers, and raccoons.
10. Some lucky visitors even spot black bears or (wolves, wolfs).
11. The (rangers', rangeres) job is to watch over the park, the animals, and the visitors.

Lesson 2.7 Compound Words

A **compound word** is made by joining two shorter words.

out + side = outside   sea + shell = seashell   sun + burn = sunburn

Use the pictures to help you fill in the blanks in the problems below.

1. [hand] + nail = _____

2. pop + [corn] = _____

3. [star] + fish = _____

4. door + [bell] = _____

5. [foot] + ball = _____

6. [horse] + back = _____

7. [sun] + flower = _____

8. [wheel] + chair = _____

On the lines below, write the two words that form each compound word.

1. _____ + _____ = notebook

2. _____ + _____ = backyard

3. _____ + _____ = sandbox

4. _____ + _____ = snowball

5. _____ + _____ = teaspoon

6. _____ + _____ = newspaper

Lesson 2.7 Compound Words

Form a common compound word by drawing a line to match each word
in column 1 to a word in column 2. Write the compound word on the line.

1. ear   food   _____

2. lawn   mill   _____

3. light   work   _____

4. sea   mower   _____

5. scare   crow   _____

6. home   ring   _____

7. wind   set   _____

8. sun   house   _____

Read the clues below. Choose the words from the box that match the
clues, and write them on the lines.

| sailboat   pinecone   newspaper   lunchroom |
| washcloth   nightgown   spaceship |

1. a room in which people eat lunch   _____

2. a cone from a pine tree   _____

3. a gown that is worn at night   _____

4. a cloth used for washing   _____

5. a paper filled with news   _____

6. a boat used for sailing   _____

7. a ship used for traveling into space   _____

Lesson 2.8 Contractions

A **contraction** is a short way of writing two words. When the words are combined, an apostrophe (') takes the place of the missing letters.

I am = I'm   he will = he'll   we have = we've   is not = isn't

The words *will* and *not* form the contraction *won't*.

Draw a line to match the words on the left with their contractions.

1. he would   I'll
2. I will   she's
3. did not   you've
4. have not   haven't
5. she is   he'd
6. they are   weren't
7. were not   didn't
8. you have   they're

Read each sentence below. On the line, write the contraction for the words in bold.

1. Julia **has not** left the house in a week. _____

2. **She is** getting over the chicken pox. _____

3. Julia's case of the chicken pox **was not** as bad as Max's was. _____

4. **He will** be back in school next week, too. _____

5. Julia's mom told her she **should not** scratch too hard. _____

6. "**That is** easier said than done!" replied Julia. _____

Lesson 2.8 Contractions

Fill in the blanks to complete the problems below. Some problems have more than one correct answer. For example, **'d** can stand for *had* or *would*.

1. we + _____ = we're   6. it + _____ = it's

2. _____ + not = won't   7. _____ + not = couldn't

3. I + am = _____   8. I + have = _____

4. they + _____ = they'd   9. you + _____ = you're

5. she + has = _____   10. _____ + is = he's

Read the riddles below. Circle the contraction in each riddle. Then, write the two words that form the contraction.

1. **Q:** What did one eye say to the other?

   A: Don't look down, but something smells.

   _____ _____

2. **Q:** What runs around a house but doesn't move?

   A: A fence. _____ _____

3. **Q:** Why do hens lay eggs?

   A: Because if they dropped them, they'd break.

   _____ _____

4. **Q:** What kind of bird can't swim, fly, or catch a fish?

   A: A peli-can't. _____ _____

5. **Q:** What's the capital in France?

   A: F. _____ _____

Lesson 2.8 Contractions

Read the sentences below. On the line, write the contraction from the box that best completes each sentence.

haven't	We've	won't	I'm	they're	He'll	It's

1. _____ going to the movies on Saturday night with my best friend, Eduardo.

2. _____ ride his bike to my house on Saturday afternoon.

3. We _____ ever been to a drive-in movie before.

4. My mom says _____ much more fun than regular movies.

5. _____ packed a bag with snacks and drinks.

6. _____ going to be a double feature.

7. We _____ get home until almost midnight!

In each sentence below, there are two words that can be combined to form a contraction. Circle the words and write the contraction on the line.

1. Who is your favorite actor?   _____

2. We will meet you outside the theater at 3:00.   _____

3. I can not remember the name of the movie.   _____

4. Izzy has not seen the movie yet.   _____

5. She has been going to at least one movie
   a week for as long as she can remember.   _____

6. Taylor doesn't like scary movies, so he would
   not like *The Mystery of the Missing Hand.*   _____

Lesson 2.8 Contractions

Read the contractions below. On the first line, write the two words that form the contraction. On the second line, write the letters replaced by the apostrophe.

1. they've _____ ____
2. what's _____ ____
3. we're _____ ____
4. didn't _____ ____
5. let's _____ ____

6. that's _____ ____
7. I'm _____ ____
8. shouldn't _____ ____
9. she'll _____ ____
10. would've _____ ____

Read the silly sentences below. On each line, write the contraction for the words in parentheses.

1. Sheila _____ share sugar cookies with Shane and Shawn. (should not)

2. _____ wild, wacky, and weird on Wednesdays. (We are)

3. _____ eaten ice cream in the igloo with Ida and Isaac. (I have)

4. Willy and Wendy _____ worry when we whisper. (will not)

5. _____ dip the dumplings in the dumpling dip, Donna. (do not)

6. Cassidy _____ kept the carpet clean with caution and care. (could have)

Phonics Connection

What are the three digraphs used in the first exercise above?

_____   _____   _____

Review Compound Words and Contractions

Look at the pictures below. Choose the compound word from the box that names each picture, and write it on the line.

rainbow	bedroom	teacup	anteater	waterfall
cupcake	airplane	motorcycle	backpack	

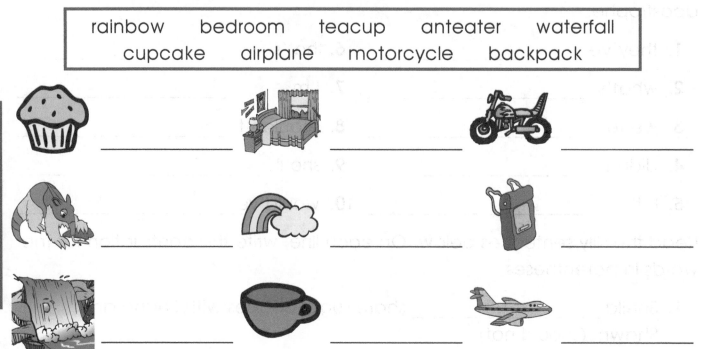

Combine each word in bold with as many of the words in the box as you can to create compound words. Write the words on the lines. Hint: The words in bold will be the first part of each compound.

works	flake	brush	bath	seat	shine	yard	burn
paste	fly	cage	bone	place	rise	storm	seed

1. **back** _____ _____ _____

2. **bird** _____ _____ _____

3. **fire** _____ _____ _____

4. **sun** _____ _____ _____

5. **snow** _____ _____

6. **tooth** _____ _____

Review Compound Words and Contractions

Read the instructions below. Circle the six contractions. Underline the six different compound words.

Make a Homemade Windmill

Here's what you will need:

- a pencil with an eraser
- a ruler
- a square sheet of paper
- scissors
- a thumbtack

1. Draw a circle about two inches wide in the center of the piece of paper. Make a dot in the center of the circle.

2. Cut a straight line from each corner of the paper to the circle. Don't cut into the circle.

3. Bend every other point to the dot you drew in the center of the circle. It's important that the paper doesn't get folded when you bend it.

4. Hold the points together. Have a grownup stick the thumbtack through the points of paper and the center of the circle.

5. Push the tip of the thumbtack into the pencil eraser. The tack shouldn't be pushed all the way into the eraser.

6. When you blow gently on your windmill, it'll turn. Can you think of something other than wind that might be able to power a mill outside?

Lesson 2.9 Prefixes

A **prefix** can be added to the beginning of some words. Adding a prefix changes the meaning of a word.

• The prefixes **un-** and **dis-** both mean *not*.

uneven = not even   **dis**honest = not honest

Add the prefix in parentheses ( ) to each base word below. Write the new word on the first line. On the second line, write the definition of the word.

1. (un) able   _____ _____

2. (dis) agree   _____ _____

3. (dis) like   _____ _____

4. (un) sure   _____ _____

5. (un) equal   _____ _____

6. (dis) trust   _____ _____

Add a prefix to each word below. Write the new word on the line. Then, write a sentence using the word you formed.

1. un + pack = _____

_____

2. dis + appear = _____

_____

3. un + plug = _____

_____

4. dis + obey = _____

_____

Lesson 2.9 Prefixes

> • The prefixes **in-** and **im-** can mean *not.*
>
> **in**direct = not direct   **im**perfect = not perfect

Draw a line to match each word in column 1 with its definition in column 2.

1. impolite	not patient
2. incorrect	not complete
3. invisible	not correct
4. impatient	not possible
5. inexpensive	not polite
6. impossible	not exact
7. incomplete	not expensive
8. inexact	not visible

Read the sentences below. On the line, write a word from the box that best completes the sentence.

> impolite   indoors   impossible   incorrect   indirect   impure

1. Our plant needs _____ light, so don't put it directly in the sun.

2. It is _____ not to thank someone who holds a door open.

3. The scientist cannot use water that is _____ in her experiments.

4. Only one of your answers on the test was _____.

5. Please do not roller-skate _____!

6. If you believe in yourself, nothing in the world is _____.

Lesson 2.9   Prefixes

> • The prefix **re-** can mean *again*.
>
>   **re**do = do again   **re**paint = paint again
>
> • The prefix **pre-** means *before*.
>
>   **pre**heat = heat before   **pre**pay = pay before
>
> • The prefix **mis-** means *wrongly* or *badly*.
>
>   **mis**match = match wrongly   **mis**lead = lead badly

Read each definition below. Think of a matching word with the prefix **re-**, **pre-**, or **mis-** and write it on the line.

1. order before = _____

2. pack again = _____

3. read wrongly = _____

4. wash before = _____

5. check again = _____

6. mix before = _____

7. judge wrongly = _____

Add a prefix to each base word below. Write the new word on the first line. On the second line, write the definition of the word.

1. re + count = _____   _____

2. pre + dawn = _____   _____

3. mis + connect = _____   _____

4. pre + cook = _____   _____

5. re + sell = _____   _____

6. mis + name = _____   _____

Lesson 2.9 Prefixes

- The prefix **over-** means *too much.*
  overpay = pay too much   **over**flow = flow too much
- The prefix **under-** means *too little* or *below.*
  undercook = cook too little   **under**shirt = shirt worn below

Read the clues below. Each answer will contain the prefix **over-** or **under-**. Write your answer on the line.

1. The opposite of *undercharge* is _____.

2. The opposite of *overweight* is _____.

3. The opposite of *overdress* is _____.

4. The opposite of *undercook* is _____.

5. The opposite of *overrate* is _____.

6. The opposite of *undersize* is _____.

Read each sentence below. On the line, write a word from the box to take the place of the words in bold.

overslept underground overthink overrated underwater underline

1. Can you open your eyes **below the water**?   _____

2. The last book I read was **rated too high**.   _____

3. Put a **line below** each compound word.   _____

4. Do not **think too much** about your answer.   _____

5. Brandon's alarm did not go off, so he
   slept too much.   _____

6. The mole burrowed into its hole **below the ground**. _____

Lesson 2.10 Suffixes

Suffixes can be added to the ends of some words. A suffix changes the meaning of the word to which it is added.

• The suffix **-ly** means *in a way*. If a base word ends in **y**, change the **y** to **i** before adding **ly**.

slow**ly** = in a slow way   happy → happ**ily** = in a happy way

• The suffix **-y** means *being* or *having*. If a base word ends in **e**, drop the **e** before adding **y**.

thirst**y** = having thirst   slime → slim**y** = having slime

Add the suffix in parentheses ( ) to each base word below. Use the new word in a sentence.

1. mess (y) _____

2. quick (ly) _____

3. bounce (y) _____

4. soft (ly) _____

5. easy (ly) _____

6. luck (y) _____

Read the definitions below. On the line, write the word that matches each definition.

1. in a strong way_____   **4.** having tricks _____

2. having rust _____   **5.** having steam _____

3. in a safe way _____   **6.** in a noisy way _____

Lesson 2.10 Suffixes

• The suffixes **-er** and **-or** can mean *a person who.*

writ**er** = a person who writes   act**or** = a person who acts

Read the sentences below. On the line, write a word with the suffix **-er** or **-or** to take the place of the words in bold.

1. When Carmen grows up, she hopes to be
   a person who teaches.   _____

2. Jill loves art class and knows that she will
   be **a person who paints**.   _____

3. Bailey lives near the ocean and plans to
   become **a person who sails**.   _____

4. Amina has hundreds of ideas for new things to
   make, so she wants to be **a person who invents**.   _____

5. Oliver's family has lived on a farm for 90 years,
   so he will be **a person who farms**.   _____

6. Andy dreams of being **a person who governs**.   _____

Write the meaning of each word on the line beside it.

1. sculptor = _____

2. collector = _____

3. gardener = _____

4. builder = _____

5. runner = _____

Lesson 2.10 Suffixes

- The suffix **-ful** means *full of*. If a base word ends in **y**, change the **y** to **i** before adding **ful**.

  room**ful** = a room full of   beauti**ful** = full of beauty

- The suffix **-less** means *without*.

  color**less** = without color   end**less** = without end

Read the clues below. Choose the word from the box that matches each clue. Write the answers in the numbered spaces in the crossword puzzle.

tasteful hopeless joyful careless peaceful spotless painless thankful

Across

2. without pain
4. full of thanks
7. without hope

Down

1. full of peace
3. without spots
4. full of taste
5. without care
6. full of joy

Lesson 2.10   Suffixes

- The suffix **-able** means *can be* or *able to be*. If a base word ends in **e**, drop the **e** before adding **able**.

  enjoy**able** = able to be enjoyed   use → us**able** = able to be used

- The suffix **-en** means *made of* or *to make*. If a base word ends in **e**, drop the **e** before adding **en**. For words that have a short vowel sound and end in a consonant, double the consonant before adding **en**.

  bright**en** = to make bright   loose → loos**en** = to make loose
  mad → madd**en** = to make mad

Read the sentences below. Add the suffix **-able** or **-en** to each word in parentheses ( ) so that it correctly completes the sentence.

1. The toy is made of soft plastic, so it is _____. (bend)

2. Be careful! Those plates are _____. (break)

3. Did Kayla find the _____ coins? (hid)

4. Doing pushups every day will _____ your muscles. (strength)

5. The _____ CD is on the desk. (broke)

Add a suffix to each base word below. Write the new word on the first line. On the second line, write the definition of the word.

1. hard + en = _____   _____

2. love + able = _____   _____

3. wash + able = _____   _____

4. wide + en = _____   _____

5. sharp + en = _____   _____

Review Prefixes and Suffixes

Adding a **prefix** to the beginning of a word can change the word's meaning.
- **un-, dis-, in-, im-** = not (**un**sure) • **re-** = again (**re**start)
- **pre-** = before (**pre**school) • **mis-** = wrongly or badly (**mis**read)
- **over-** = too much (**over**cook) • **under-** = too little (**under**cook)

Beside each word, write the letter of its definition.

1. _____ invisible

2. _____ overcharge

3. _____ uneven

4. _____ refill

5. _____ preorder

6. _____ disagree

a. charge too much

b. not even

c. order before

d. not agree

e. not visible

f. fill again

Read the sentences below. Circle the word from the pair in parentheses ( ) that best completes each sentence.

1. The explorer Roald Amundsen was (undone, unafraid) of new challenges.

2. At first, he planned to explore the North Pole. He (removed, rethought) his plan when others got there first.

3. Amundsen (premixed, prearranged) a group of people who would travel with him.

4. The explorers packed everything they would need. They were careful not to (overload, overflow) themselves.

5. They were (unsure, unhealthy) if they would be first to reach the South Pole.

6. Amundsen was careful not to (mislead, misname) his group.

Review   Prefixes and Suffixes

> Adding a **suffix** to the end of a word can change the meaning of the word. Remember, sometimes the spelling of words that end in **y** or **e** must change before the suffix can be added.
> - **-ly** = in a way (quick**ly**)
> - **-er, -or** = a person who (writ**er**)
> - **-less** = without (harm**less**)
> - **-en** = made of or to make (soft**en**)
> - **-y** = being or having (mess**y**)
> - **-ful** = full of (cheer**ful**)
> - **-able** = able to be (break**able**)

Add a suffix to each word below. Write the new word on the line. Then, write a sentence using the word you formed.

1. act + or = _____

_____

2. storm + y = _____

_____

3. beauty + ful = _____

_____

4. value + able = _____

_____

Read the definitions below. Write the word that matches each definition.

1. in a sleepy way _____

2. without end _____

3. to make dark _____

4. able to be fixed _____

5. a person who leads _____

Lesson 2.11　Syllables

A **syllable** is part of a word and has one vowel sound. As you say a word, listen to the number of vowel sounds. This is the number of syllables the word has.

book = 1 vowel sound = 1 syllable
pic·ture = 2 vowel sounds = 2 syllables
for·ev·er = 3 vowel sounds = 3 syllables

Look at each picture below. Choose the word from the box that names the picture and write it on the first line. On the second line, write the number of vowel sounds you hear when you say the word out loud.

| bicycle | monkey | tree |
| kangaroo | pretzel | balloon |

Phonics Connection

1. Which two picture names have the vowel sound you hear in *goose*?

_____　　　_____

2. Which two picture names begin with a two-letter blend?
Circle the blend.

_____　　　_____

Lesson 2.11 Syllables

> Compound words can be divided into syllables between the two parts of the compound.
>
> cup·cake   book·case
>
> A word that has two consonants between two vowels (like ba**sk**e_t_) can be divided between the consonants.
>
> pen·cil   nap·kin
>
> A word that has a prefix can be divided between the prefix and the base word.
>
> pre·wash   mis·count

Read each word below. Say it to yourself and listen for the vowel sounds. Draw a slash (/) to divide each word into syllables.

1. airplane
2. dislike
3. picture
4. cookbook
5. refill

6. bathtub
7. beehive
8. preheat
9. lumber
10. undo

Read the sentences below. Use slashes to divide the words in bold into syllables.

1. On **Monday**, Cal went to the **dentist** because he had a **toothache**.
2. It was **winter**, so Cal could see his **footprints** in the snow on the **sidewalk**.
3. The **sunlight** was bright, and Cal was eager to get **indoors**.
4. "**Welcome** to Dr. Garcia's office," **someone** said.
5. Cal **untied** his boots and left them in the **hallway**.
6. He **disliked** cavities, but he loved going to Dr. Garcia's **office**.

Lesson 2.11 Syllables

Read the words in the box. Write each word below the correct heading.
Then, draw slashes (/) to divide the words into syllables.

> cucumber wind seashore unlock wonderful bench
> popular shrimp table fish star terrible
> ladder breeze adventure silent homesick elephant

1 syllable	**2 syllables**	**3 syllables**
_____	_____	_____
_____	_____	_____
_____	_____	_____
_____	_____	_____
_____	_____	_____
_____	_____	_____

Read each word in bold. Circle the word beside it that has the same
number of syllables.

1. **grassy**	sniff	mitten	however
2. **difficult**	vacation	puzzle	jolly
3. **whale**	railroad	monster	sled
4. **pocket**	bush	before	bike
5. **multiply**	flavor	drive	factory
6. **cry**	pinch	different	fastest
7. **pumpkin**	paper	banana	climb
8. **water**	multiply	closed	hammer
9. **stomp**	trying	loose	crocodile

Lesson 2.11 Syllables

Read the sentences below. The words in parentheses ( ) will tell you which words to underline in the sentences.

1. When Hurricane Katrina hit the U.S. in 2005, it did a lot of damage. (3-syllable words)

2. Many people around the world wanted to help. (2-syllable words)

3. Three sisters in Maryland thought of a very special way to make a difference. (3-syllable words)

4. They started Project Backpack. (2-syllable words)

5. Jackie, Melissa, and Jenna Kantor collected backpacks full of things that kids along the Gulf Coast might need. (2-syllable words)

6. They quickly reached their goal of 1,000 backpacks. (1-syllable words)

7. Kids around the country heard about the project. (2-syllable words)

8. They collected backpacks in their own cities, too. (1-syllable words)

9. In two months, 50,000 backpacks were sent to kids who lived in the areas Katrina hit! (3-syllable words)

10. Even though the Kantor sisters were only 14, 11, and 8, they helped thousands of kids they had never even met. (2-syllable words)

Phonics Connection

1. Which word in number 2 has a **y** that makes the long **e** sound? _____

2. Which word in number 5 has the same vowel sound as *blow*? _____

3. Which word in number 6 has the hard **g** sound? _____

Review Syllables

Choose the word from the box that names each picture below and write it on the first line. On the second line, write the number of vowel sounds you hear when you say the word out loud.

| mosquito | banana | mailbox | pear | snowflake | wink |

Read the words below and fill in the blanks in the chart.

	Vowel Sounds Heard	Number of Syllables
rosebush		
crash		
misjudge		
redraw		
difficult		
washcloth		
crocodile		
plate		
pretzel		
corner		

Review Syllables

On the line, write the word that names the picture. Then, circle the word beside it that has the same number of syllables.

1. _____ curious   insect   book

2. _____ rug   water   valley

3. _____ plug   notebook listening

4. _____ tiger   bowl   area

5. _____ forever   fastest   ring

Read the paragraphs below. Use slashes (/) to divide the words in bold into syllables.

A **cactus** is a type of plant. It grows **mostly** in desert **areas** of the Americas. Cacti (the plural of cactus) are one of few plants that can live in the harsh **conditions** of deserts. **Unlike** most plants, cacti do not have leaves. **Instead**, they have sharp spines. The spines **protect** cacti from **desert animals**. Since plants usually lose **water** through their leaves, the spines help cacti save their water. Cacti also have thick, **fleshy** stems where they can store water. Their roots do not go deep **into** the ground like **other** plants. Instead, they spread out **over** a large space so they can get water from a **wider** area when it rains.

There are **about** 1,700 **species** of cacti. One of the most interesting may be the saguaro cactus. It lives in the **Southwest** and in **Mexico** and can grow to be 50 feet tall!

Lesson 3.1 Synonyms

A **synonym** is a word that has the same or almost the same meaning as another word.

like, enjoy   dad, father   quick, fast   insect, bug

Look at each picture and label below. Find the word in the box that is a synonym for the picture name, and write it on the line.

| rabbit | present | rip | pail | hat | smile |

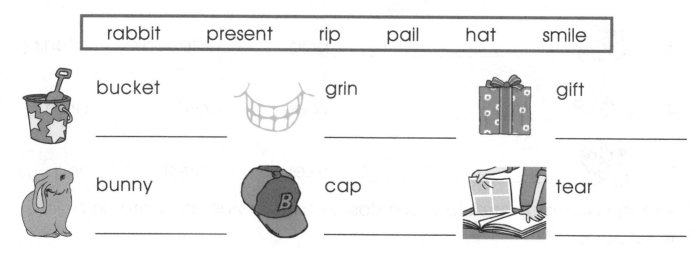

bucket

_____

grin

_____

gift

_____

bunny

_____

cap

_____

tear

_____

Read each clue and the choices below it. Circle the word that best matches the clue.

1. I am another word for *great* or *wonderful*.

    awful   terrific   old

2. I am another word for *tired*.

    sleepy   worried   joyful

3. I am another word for *huge* or *enormous*.

    tiny   slippery   giant

4. I am another word for *wreck*.

    move   push   destroy

5. I am another word for *laugh*.

    giggle   sigh   scream

Lesson 3.1 Synonyms

Draw a line to match each word in column 1 to its synonym in column 2.

1. end		beautiful
2. easy		mend
3. shut		near
4. pretty		finish
5. throw		simple
6. glad		close
7. jump		hop
8. close		toss
9. fix		happy

Read each sentence below. Find a synonym in the box for the word in bold and write it on the line.

see quiet pick broke small stop scream keep tug

1. **Choose** your three favorite flavors. _____

2. Tell Marissa to **pull** on the rope. _____

3. The house is **silent** in the middle of the night. _____

4. When did you **quit** taking ballet lessons? _____

5. The plate **shattered** when it hit the floor. _____

6. When Olivia walks we'll **shout** "Surprise!" _____

7. The sliver was so **tiny** I could barely see it. _____

8. Did you **watch** the game on TV last night? _____

9. Let's **save** the rest of the brownies for later. _____

Lesson 3.2 Antonyms

An **antonym** is a word that means the opposite of another word.

hard, soft   loud, quiet   new, old   right, wrong

Read the clues below. Fill in the blanks to complete the answer. Then, look for each answer in the word search puzzle. Circle the words you find.

1. the opposite of *top*   b____ ____ ____ ____ ____

2. the opposite of *black*   wh____ ____ ____

3. the opposite of *enemy*   fr____ ____ ____ ____

4. the opposite of *evening*   m____ ____ ____ ____ ____ ____

5. the opposite of *up*   d____ ____ ____

6. the opposite of *love*   h____ ____ ____

7. the opposite of *over*

    u____ ____ ____ ____

Phonics Connection

1. Which puzzle word contains a digraph?

   _____

2. Which puzzle word has a beginning blend?

   _____

n	m	r	u	n	d	e	r	v	a
q	d	b	b	j	a	r	h	p	l
b	o	t	t	o	m	c	a	z	x
o	w	p	l	y	o	e	t	g	i
j	n	u	n	f	r	i	e	n	d
s	d	r	t	n	n	q	o	a	p
d	g	m	w	h	i	t	e	w	n
r	z	t	t	w	n	o	u	n	h
e	g	c	f	e	g	r	h	n	e

Lesson 3.2 Antonyms

Read the paragraphs below. Choose an antonym from the box for each word in bold. Write it on the line beside the word.

slower	less	finished	bad	lost	easy
weaker	woman	short	smaller	fake	boring

American **tall** _____ tales were begun by pioneers of the Old West. Tall tales were a **good** _____ form of entertainment. TV did not exist, and books were **hard** _____ to get. Tall tales could be told to a group and passed from one person to the next. The main character of a tall tale is often someone who is **larger** _____ than life. The character is superhuman in some way and has wild adventures. In the story, he or she may be **stronger** _____, **faster** _____, smarter, or tougher than anyone else.

For example, have you ever heard the tale of John Henry? He could hammer railroad spikes faster than any **man** _____. He was **more** _____ than eight feet tall when he was born. He **started** _____ working on the railways when he was only three weeks old. When he raced against a machine, John Henry **won** _____. The tall tale is funnier and more interesting than the **real** _____ story could ever be.

Paul Bunyan, Annie Oakley, and Johnny Appleseed are other tall tale heroes you might know. What details make their stories so **exciting** _____?

Review Synonyms and Antonyms

Read each pair of words below. If the words are synonyms, write **S** on the line. If they are antonyms, write **A**.

1. _____ yell, whisper

2. _____ shout, scream

3. _____ easy, simple

4. _____ heavy, light

5. _____ like, enjoy

6. _____ wide, narrow

7. _____ funny, serious

8. _____ boat, ship

9. _____ tired, sleepy

10. _____ inside, outside

11. _____ city, town

12. _____ summer, winter

The word in parentheses ( ) will tell you to find a synonym or an antonym for each word below. Choose your answer from the box and write it on the line.

| noisy full smooth lost west wrong infant find messy ill |

1. neat (antonym) _____

2. empty (antonym) _____

3. missing (synonym) _____

4. sick (synonym) _____

5. right (antonym) _____

6. baby (synonym) _____

7. east (antonym) _____

8. loud (synonym) _____

9. locate (synonym) _____

10. rough (antonym) _____

Review Synonyms and Antonyms

Read the paragraphs below. Then, answer the questions that follow.

Have you ever visited a corn maze? The largest corn maze in the country is at the Richardson Farm in Spring Grove, Illinois. Every year, the family picks a new theme. An artist makes a drawing that goes with the theme. Then, the picture gets scanned into a computer. The lines of the picture are turned into the maze. When the corn on the farm is ten inches tall, the maze is cut into the fields. It's easier to cut the corn before it grows too tall.

In autumn, the Richardsons are ready for their first visitors to the maze. In 2004, the maze had pictures from Lewis and Clark's journey. In ten miles of trails, there were pictures of prairie dogs, bison (or buffaloes), and a traveler in a boat. Even though the trails are about ten miles long, you only have to walk about $\frac{1}{3}$ of a mile to solve a maze. What happens if you get lost? Don't worry, you'll be able to bring a map with you. You can also bring a cell phone to call the Richardsons for help if you get stuck.

1. Find an antonym for *smallest* in paragraph 1. _____

2. Find a synonym for *nation* in paragraph 1. _____

3. Find an antonym for *old* in paragraph 1. _____

4. Find a synonym for *creates* in paragraph 1. _____

5. Find an antonym for *harder* in paragraph 1. _____

6. Find an antonym for *shrinks* in paragraph 1. _____

7. Find a synonym for *fall* in paragraph 2. _____

8. Find an antonym for *last* in paragraph 2. _____

9. Find an antonym for *short* in paragraph 2. _____

10. Find an antonym for *found* in paragraph 2. _____

Lesson 3.3 Homophones

A **homophone** is a word that sounds the same as another word but has a different spelling and meaning.

It takes an *hour* to get there. *Our* team won the game!

Tom will *be* late. The *bee* landed on the pink flower.

Circle the word below each picture that correctly names it. Use a dictionary if you are not sure which homophone to choose.

bear bare

shoo shoe

I eye

eight ate

pear pair

son sun

knight night

flour flower

ant aunt

Phonics Connection

There are three words in the exercise above that have a silent consonant pair. Write the words on the lines and circle the consonant pair in each word.

_____   _____   _____

Lesson 3.3 Homophones

Read each sentence below. The word in parentheses ( ) is a homophone for the word in bold. Write a sentence of your own using the homophone.

Example: Did Courtney **write** a story?

(right) Make a right turn at the light.

1. I **sent** Grandma an e-mail last week.

(cent) _____

2. What kind of **clothes** are you wearing to the party?

(close) _____

3. Alejandro will **meet** you at the park at noon.

(meat) _____

4. **Here** is the book I borrowed from you.

(hear) _____

Read the clues below. On the first line, write the word from box 1 that matches the clue. Then, find its homophone in box 2 and write it on the second line.

road bye they're high four	hi there buy for rode

1. I am what people say when they are leaving.

_____ _____

2. I am the number that comes after three. _____ _____

3. I am the opposite of *low*. _____ _____

4. I am another name for *street*. _____ _____

5. I am a contraction for *they are*. _____ _____

Lesson 3.4 Multiple-Meaning Words

A **multiple-meaning word** (also called a **homograph**) is a word that has more than one meaning.

Can you help us?   George bought a *can* of tuna.

Mia won the doll at the *fair*.   It's not *fair* that you have to go last.

Read each sentence below. On the line, write a sentence using another meaning of the word in bold. If you cannot think of another meaning, use a dictionary.

1. Did you drive or **fly** to Chicago?

   _____

2. The **bat** eats hundreds of mosquitoes every night.

   _____

3. The owl's wings are almost the same color as the **bark** of the tree.

   _____

4. On their first **date**, Abby's parents went to the movies.

   _____

5. Mrs. Kay needs one **yard** of fabric to make the costume.

   _____

6. We were late for school because we got stuck in a traffic **jam**.

   _____

7. How many pigs did you count in the **pen**?

   _____

8. Darren's dad works in a three-**story** building.

   _____

Lesson 3.4 Multiple-Meaning Words

Read each sentence and the definitions that follow. Circle the letter of the definition that matches the word in bold.

1. Nicholas and Matthew bought their dad a **watch** for his birthday.

   a. to look at   **b.** a small clock worn on the wrist

2. There is a **pitcher** of lemonade on the counter.

   a. a container that holds liquid   **b.** the person who pitches

3. Sanj's cold is gone and she feels **fine**.

   a. well; in good health   **b.** money paid for breaking a law

4. The dentist gave Eric a pack of sugar-free **gum**.

   a. the flesh around your teeth   **b.** a type of rubbery candy

5. The **kind** woman works at an animal shelter.

   a. nice; gentle; helpful   **b.** a type or sort

6. A huge gust of **wind** knocked over the sign.

   a. to tighten by turning   **b.** blowing air

7. How **close** is your school to your home?

   a. to shut   **b.** near

8. Gabby came in **second** in the race.

   a. number two   **b.** a measurement of time

Phonics Connection

Use the words in bold above to answer the following questions.

1. Which two words have the long **i** sound?

   _____   _____

2. Which two words have a silent consonant? Circle the consonant.

   _____   _____

Lesson 3.5 Figures of Speech

A **simile** is a comparison of two unlike things using the words *like* or *as*.
Lydia's *cheeks* were *as red as cherries*.
The sea sparkled *like jewels* in the morning sun.
A **metaphor** is a comparison of two unlike things without using *like* or *as*.
Alexander's *heart* was *a steady drum* beating in his chest.

Read each sentence below. If it contains a simile, write **S** on the line. If it contains a metaphor, write **M**.

1. _____ By dinnertime, Katsu will be as hungry as a bear.

2. _____ The tornado was a roaring train that sped across the field.

3. _____ Charlotte was a dolphin, diving and playing in the waves.

4. _____ Annie's new ideas were a breath of fresh air.

5. _____ The windows were like eyes that peered out from the front of the house.

6. _____ Jake's dry hands were as rough as sandpaper.

7. _____ The fog was a blanket that covered the sleeping city.

8. _____ The water felt like ice to C. J. as he dove into the pool.

Use your imagination to complete each simile below.

1. Kelsey's eyes are as green as _____.

2. The lemon juice stung like _____ on Iman's paper cut.

3. The raspberries from the garden were as sweet as _____.

4. The pebbles were as smooth as _____ in Xavier's hand.

Lesson 3.5 Figures of Speech

Read the paragraphs below. Underline the four similes. Circle the two metaphors.

Fiona and Nora walked down the sandy path to the beach. It was the middle of the day, and the sand felt like hot coals under their bare feet. They walked faster, trying not to let their feet touch the sand for long. The water was a blue carpet stretching out toward the sky. It looked cool and inviting from the hot beach.

"It's beautiful here, isn't it?" said Nora. She turned her face to the sun that hung like a fat, yellow grapefruit in the sky. Nora sniffed the salty breeze. "The ocean air smells as fresh as clean laundry."

The girls found their parents and spread out their towels. They were careful not to wake their dad, who slept like a baby under a large umbrella. Suddenly, Fiona spotted a pelican. It was a missile zooming toward the water. A moment later, it flew away with a wriggling fish sticking out of its beak. "There's always something going on at the beach!" laughed Fiona.

Read the metaphors below. On the lines, tell which two things are being compared.

1. The 175-year-old house was a dinosaur.

_____   _____

2. The stomachs of the teenage boys were bottomless pits.

_____   _____

3. Marcus's legs were rubber as he walked onstage.

_____   _____

Review Homophones, Multiple-Meaning Words, Figures of Speech

Circle the word below each picture that correctly names it. Use a dictionary if you are not sure which homophone to choose.

hair   hare   hoarse   horse   be   bee

dear   deer   ring   wring   mussel   muscle

Read each sentence below. Circle the homophone that correctly completes the sentence.

1. The department store is having a (sail, sale) on kids' clothes this week.
2. (Meat, Meet) me at the car in one (hour, our).
3. The mountain (peak, peek) is 1,700 feet above sea level.
4. (Your, You're) book report is really interesting.

Read the pairs of homophones below. Use each one in a sentence.

1. (wood, would) _____

   _____

2. (one, won) _____

   _____

3. (plain, plane) _____

   _____

Review Homophones, Multiple-Meaning Words, Figures of Speech

Read the definitions and the sentences below. Make a check mark beside the sentence that uses the word in bold the same way as the definition.

1. tear = liquid that comes out of the eyes when crying

___ A **tear** rolled down the girl's cheek.   ___ Did you **tear** your shirt?

2. seal = a mammal that lives in the ocean and has flippers

___ **Seal** each letter before you mail it.   ___ The **seal** has thick, gray fur.

3. rest = to take a break or relax

___ Where are the **rest** of the children?   ___ **Rest** quietly until lunch.

4. well = a hole dug in the ground to get to water

___ We never use the old **well** in the yard. ___ **Well**, I'm ready to go.

5. box = a square container

___ My uncle likes to **box** at the gym.   ___ What's inside the **box**?

Read each sentence below. Circle the two things that are being compared. Write **S** on the line if the comparison is a simile. Write **M** if it is a metaphor.

1. _____ The rain sounded like tiny footsteps racing across the roof.

2. _____ "Britta is the apple of my eye," said Grandpa proudly.

3. _____ The snow was a thick, white blanket on the rooftop.

4. _____ The heavy meal sat like a rock in Mr. Bloomberg's stomach.

5. _____ The children were quiet as mice as they waited.

Phonics Connection

Which three words in exercise 2 have the long **e** sound spelled **y**?

_____   _____   _____

Lesson 4.1 Alphabetical Order

Being able to place words in **alphabetical order**, or **ABC order**, can help you find what you are looking for in a dictionary, an encyclopedia, an index, or at the library.

When two words start with the same letter, use the second letter to decide the order. If the first two letters of the words are the same, use the third letter.

habit **j**eep **l**amb   **pa**sta **pe**st **pi**e   **da**rling **da**sh **da**te

Read each set of words. On the lines, number the words in ABC order.

1. _____ train   3. _____ ear   5. _____ list

   _____ uncle   _____ explain   _____ kitten

   _____ piano   _____ ever   _____ king

2. _____ paste   4. _____ hem   6. _____ mimic

   _____ pass   _____ hey   _____ mint

   _____ phase   _____ herd   _____ milk

Rewrite each list below so the words are in ABC order.

1. minnow, line, hers, mile _____

2. sloth, skunk, sleigh, sled _____

3. news, net, niece, nibble _____

Phonics Connection

1. Which word in exercise 1 begins with a digraph? _____

2. Which three words in exercise 2 begin with an **l** blend?

_____   _____   _____

Lesson 4.1 Alphabetical Order

Erica and Jamal are going to the library. They have a list of books to find. Fill in the blanks on their list with titles from the box. Make sure that the list stays in ABC order. Hint: Ignore the word *the* at the beginning of book titles.

The Bears on Hemlock Mountain

_____

Charlie and the Chocolate Factory

_____

Coyote Steals the Blanket
Exploring the Deep, Dark Sea
Fantastic Mr. Fox
The Gadget War

_____

_____

How to Eat Fried Worms
If a Bus Could Talk: The Story of Rosa Parks
Leonardo's Horse

_____

The Pirate's Handbook
Ramona Quimby, Age 8
Sarah, Plain and Tall

_____

Stuart Little

_____

Zathura

Squids Will Be Squids

The House of Wisdom

High as a Hawk

Piggins

Coming on Home Soon

Superfudge

Bloomers!

Lesson 4.2 Guide Words

Guide words are words that appear at the top of a dictionary page. They tell you the first and last word on that page of the dictionary. If the word you are searching for comes between the guide words in ABC order, it will be on that page of the dictionary.

For example, *bagel* would be on the page with the guide words *badly* and *bail* because it comes between them in ABC order.

Read each set of guide words below. Circle the word that would appear on a dictionary page with them.

1. forgave • format   forty   fork   frail
2. dial • different   dice   dig   dinosaur
3. pillow • pipe   pilgrim   plaid   pink
4. hero • hickory   heather   herself   hello
5. window • wise   wing   wish   willow

Look up each of the following words in a dictionary. On the line, write the guide words from the page on which you found the word.

1. blink _____ _____
2. soccer _____ _____
3. coin _____ _____
4. avenue _____ _____
5. horseshoe _____ _____

Phonics Connection

Which five words in exercise 1 have the /or/ sound spelled **or**?

_____ _____ _____

_____ _____

Lesson 4.2 Guide Words

Each heading below is a set of guide words from a dictionary page. Write the words from the box under the correct headings.

| blame ballet base balloon black blade barrel bamboo |
| barn band blanket balmy batch blast basket |

ball • bandage

_____

_____

_____

_____

_____

bark • bath

_____

_____

_____

_____

_____

bit • blaze

_____

_____

_____

_____

_____

Read each word below. Use the pair of guide words to decide on which dictionary page you would find the word. Write the page number on the line.

| dash • deal page 84 | dear • decoy page 85 | pick • pill page 220 | pinto • pizza page 222 |

1. picnic _____

2. date _____

3. decode _____

4. pita _____

5. deck _____

6. pigtail _____

7. dawn _____

8. pitcher _____

9. decide _____

10. pity _____

11. pierce _____

12. debt _____

13. dead _____

14. pirate _____

15. pie _____

16. daze _____

17. decay _____

18. pioneer _____

Lesson 4.3 Entry Words

When you look up a word in a dictionary, you are looking up an **entry word**. An entry word is usually printed in bold. Most entry words appear with listed endings. For example, you would look up the word *country*, not *countries*; *stop*, not *stopping*; and *smile*, not *smiled*.

entry word   pronunciation & syllables   part of speech   meaning

freckle (frek′ ul) *noun* a small brown dot on the skin, often the face

Read each word below. On the line beside it, write the entry word you would look for in a dictionary.

1. lessons _____   7. foxes _____

2. hiding _____   8. tripped _____

3. activities _____   9. carries _____

4. wrapped _____   10. laughing _____

5. scolds _____   11. thinner _____

6. hungrily _____   12. washed _____

Use the dictionary entry below to answer the questions.

pupil (pyoo pul) **1.** *noun* a student; a young person taught in a school
          2. *noun* the eye opening that allows light to enter

1. How many syllables does pupil have? _____

2. Can pupil be more than one part of speech? _____

3. Which definition of pupil is used in this sentence? Your
   pupils grow bigger when you are in a dark room. _____

Lesson 4.3 Entry Words

Read the paragraphs below. Write the entry word on the line beside each word in bold.

Julius Lester was born in Missouri in 1939. Julius's degree was in English, but he also **enjoyed** _____ music. He **recorded** _____ two albums, and he wrote a book about folk music. Later on, Julius wrote other **books** _____ for **adults** _____. They were not the books that would bring him great fame, though.

In the late 1960s, he **published** _____ two **children's** _____ books. One was called *To Be a Slave* and won an important award **called** _____ the Newbery Honor Medal. The other book was called *Black* **Folktales** _____. These two books were the start of an important **writing** _____ career for Julius Lester. So far, he has **written** _____ 25 books for **kids** _____! Most of his **stories** _____ deal with African-American history and folklore. Some of his books are *The* **Tales** _____ *of Uncle Remus, John Henry, Sam and the* **Tigers** _____, and *How Many* **Spots** _____ *Does a Leopard Have and Other Tales*.

Phonics Connection

Which two words in paragraph 1 have the same vowel sound as *sport*?

_____   _____

Review ABC Order, Guide Words, and Entry Words

Rewrite the following list of authors' names in ABC order.

Cleary, Beverly _____

Lasky, Kathryn _____

Lowry, Lois _____

White, E. B. _____

Christopher, Matt _____

Babbitt, Natalie _____

Pinkney, Jerry _____

Banks, Lynne Reid _____

Byars, Betsy _____

Dahl, Roald _____

Wallace, Bill _____

On the line, write the word that names the picture. Circle the set of guide words that you would find on the same dictionary page as the picture name.

1. _____ giggle * give   glad * globe

   glow * gold

2. _____ floppy * flute   flutter * folk

   follow * foot

3. _____ spur * sprint   spicy * spit

   sponge * sprout

Review ABC Order, Guide Words, and Entry Words

Use the dictionary entries below to answer the questions.

story (stor' ee) pl. *stories* **1.** *noun* a made-up tale that entertains people
                                                2. *noun* a floor or level of a building

spaniel (span' yul) *noun* a breed of dog that has droopy ears and silky fur

sparkle (spar' kul) *verb* to glitter or give off light

1. Put the entry words above in ABC order.

    _____   _____   _____

2. What is the plural form of *story*?   _____

3. What entry word would you use to find the
definition of *sparkling*?   _____

4. Which of the words above would you find
on a dictionary page with the guide words
stopwatch and *straw*?   _____

5. Which word is a verb?   _____

6. Which definition of *story* is used in this sentence?
Paco read his sister a story before bed.   _____

Rewrite the following words in ABC order.

1. recycle, rag, reflect, rain _____

2. cry, beach, slide, fling _____

3. feast, fan, father, fast _____

4. invite, ladybug, island, lamp _____

Answer Key

page 6
t; l; b
w; n; p

1. fan
2. book
3. fish
4. cake
5. sand
6. mail

page 7

1. dogs
2. walk
3. park
4. love
5. time
6. good

page 8
n; m; f
t, r, d

1. cat
2. skip
3. bug
4. wet
5. sag
6. shop
7. hid
8. cot

page 9
1. ss
2. ff
3. ll
4. ll; ss

5. ff; ff; ss
6. zz; ll; ss
7. ss

rat
rag
ran
rap
— cut, cup, cub, cuff
— pin, pill, pig, pit

page 10
1. HC
2. SC
3. SC
4. HC
5. SC
6. HC

1. SG
2. HG
3. SG
4. HG
5. HG
6. SG

page 11

Grocery List

grapes   celery   flour
cereal   clams   ice cream
carrots   oranges   sugar
gingerbread   milk   sliced bread
apples   lettuce   eggs
turkey   peanut butter cat food

Look at each pair of pictures. Draw a line to match the hard or soft sound to each picture.

1. soft g / hard g
2. hard c / soft c
3. hard c / soft g
4. soft c / hard g

page 12

Hard C	Soft C
collects	circle
clay	place
plastic	price
countries	
circle	

color
become
collector
club

Hard G	Soft G
glass	huge
grape	giants
games	age

page 13
1. frog
2. second
3. pencil
4. sugar
5. ice
6. cow
7. orange
8. cereal

page 14
t; b; k
ss; p; ll

1. near
2. beak
3. wings
4. hold
5. can
6. fast
7. look

page 15

1. garden — hard soft
2. gym — hard soft
3. attic — hard soft
4. case — hard soft
5. danger — hard soft
6. slice — hard soft
7. egg — hard soft
8. edge — hard soft

1. goat
2. cuddle
3. ceiling
4. geese
5. edge
6. coat

Answer Key

7. gust
8. cider
9. gel
10. crisp

page 16

1. sn
2. sk
3. sc
4. sp
5. st
6. sp
7. sw

page 17

stop; special; smoke; sniff; sky; smoke; swiftly; spark; skills

page 18

1. planets
2. slow
3. flea
4. glue
5. cloud
6. blackboard
7. closet

page 19

lock	lip	low
block	blip	blow
clock	clip	flow
flock	flip	glow
	slip	plow
		slow

1. clubhouse; Answers will vary.
2. glad; Answers will vary.
3. blue; Answers will vary.
4. floor; Answers will vary.
5. flag; Answers will vary.
6. climbed; Answers will vary.
7. sleep; Answers will vary.
8. pledge; Answers will vary.

page 20

drew; from; try; dreamed; growing; gravel; from; creeks; bright; profit; traveled; promise

1. cr
2. tr
3. cr
4. gr
5. dr
6. gr

page 21

1. grandfather
2. price
3. green
4. friend
5. broom

6. crib
7. breakfast
8. principal
9. trash
10. crawl

page 22

snake; bread; spoon
claw; drum; fly

s blend	l blend	r blend
snail	plum	fruit
smoky	slime	pretty
scooter	slipper	trunk
slime	blaze	cry
slipper	floppy	drop
skunk	glass	bring

page 23

1. Blackbirds like blueberries better than bluebirds like blackberries.   Answers will vary.
2. Mrs. Clump's class clapped when the clumsy clown climbed the cliff.   Answers will vary.
3. The French frog is friends with five fellows named Frank.   Answers will vary.
4. The skillful skunk knows how to ski, skate, skip, sketch, and skateboard.   Answers will vary.
5. The cricket and the crane crunched crispy crackers by the creek.   Answers will vary.
6. The speedy spider spun a sparkly web in space.   Answers will vary.
7. The train traveled through traffic with a troop of trucks and tractors.   Answers will vary.

Answers will vary.

page 24

1. screen	strike	scream	scold
2. straight	stray	sprout	splinter
3. spray	strong	scrape	spring
4. spl	spine	splash	streak
5. stream	scratch	straw	sprain
6. scrub	scrap	scoop	strain

str; str; scr; str; scr; str; spr; spl; str

page 25

screw; straw
sprain; street
splash; scrub

1. sprinkler

Answer Key

2. spring
3. scream
4. strawberry
5. scratch
6. strong
7. street

page 26

nt; mp; lt
nk; ft; mp

1. Mr. Flores is a scientist who works with a chimp named Moe.
2. Mr. Flores is trying to learn how animals think.
3. Moe cannot talk, but Mr. Flores spent a long time teaching him sign language.
4. Whenever Mr. Flores felt that Moe earned a reward, he gave him a plump banana.
5. Moe learned to make signs for words like drink, soft, sleep, want, and funny.
6. When Moe signs a word correctly, he jumps for joy.
7. "You're a champ, Moe," cheers Mr. Flores.

page 27

1. Next weekend, we are going to ___camp___ at the Blue Spruce State Park. (camp, damp, colt)
2. We'll sleep in our new, three-room ___tent___. (rent, tank, tent)
3. Dad said that we'll set up camp on a bed of ___soft___ pine needles. (sift, soft, salt)
4. I can't wait to ___raft___ down Spruce River. (raft, rank, craft)
5. My sister, Linh, is worried the raft will ___sink___. (wink, sent, sink)
6. My uncle ___lent___ us some lifejackets, so now Linh is excited too. (lent, tint, lamp)
7. At night, we'll ___drink___ cocoa and roast marshmallows. (dunk, drink, drift)
8. I like my marshmallows ___burnt___ to a crisp on the outside. (bent, shift, burnt)
9. Last night, I ___felt___ so excited I could hardly sleep. (felt, front, blink)
10. I just hope we don't get sprayed by a ___skunk___ like my grandpa did the last time he went camping! (slump, skunk, trunk)

page 28

ld; nd; sk
st; sk; st
nd; st; ld

c	a	s	t	l	r	b	u	p
g	n	d	d	i	h	a	n	d
q	e	g	n	b	o	l	j	o
z	s	h	i	e	l	d	a	t
d	t	v	t	u	a	s	f	b
e	r	f	l	v	i	n	l	r
s	a	n	d	h	m	a	s	k
k	o	u	l	f	d	n	t	y

page 29

1. wrist	risk	roast	wild
2. dusk	build	send	ask
3. mend	field	blind	sound
4. stand	child	grind	post
5. just	task	east	sold
6. unfold	held	hound	twist
7. wand	trust	disk	and
8. task	ask	wind	billfold

1. dentist
2. west
3. mask
4. band
5. blend
6. old
7. gold
8. disk
9. cold
10. toast

page 30

skunk   stamp   nest
honk   dump   crust

ant   belt   raft
amount   salt   left

strawberry; split; screened; stroll; street; strange; sprang; splattered; screamed; sprinted; streamed; screens; scratch; scraped

page 31

nd; ld; nd; nk; nd; st; st; nt;
nd; mp; ft; nd; st; lt; nd

page 32

sheep   chair   cherry
Answers will vary. Answers will vary. Answers will vary.

cheese   shovel   shadow
Answers will vary. Answers will vary. Answers will vary.

1. sharp
2. shark
3. cheap
4. chin

page 33

1. child
2. shine
3. chip
4. choose
5. shower
6. shade

1. ch
2. sh
3. ch
4. sh
5. sh
6. ch
7. sh
8. ch
9. ch
10. sh

page 34

thumb   phone   whale
Answers will vary. Answers will vary. Answers will vary.

Read each word in bold. Circle the digraph. Then, circle the word beside it that has the same beginning sound. If you are not sure, say the words out loud. Hint: The sounds can be the same even when the spellings are different. (Example: phase and fancy)

1. thirteen	them	thief	while
2. that	third	phonics	these
3. what	thought	wheat	thanks
4. phew	photo	whip	poster
5. thirsty	those	phony	thumb
6. whisk	throw	water	whose
7. when	when	happy	thick
8. phase	fresh	thimble	pink

page 35

Philip was a handsome white whale. He weighed thousands of pounds, but he was still a graceful swimmer. As Philip swam in giant circles, he thought about what it would be like to have a friend. All the fish in the ocean thought that Philip was too big to play with. He was lonely.

One day Philip was taking a nap in the sun when he heard a tiny whisper. "Who's there?" asked the whale, opening one huge eye. There were three tiny birds sitting on his forehead.

"I'm Theo," said one. "These are my sisters, Bella and Phoebe."

"How wonderful to have sisters!" said Philip. "Whatever you do, you always have two friends."

"We have three more sisters at home," said Theo. "I'd show you a photo but it's a little wet here."

"I'm very glad to meet you, of course," said Philip. "But what are you doing in the middle of the ocean?"

"We're looking for adventure," said Phoebe. "We want to make friends and see the whole world. Do you think you might like to join us?"

Philip laughed. He thumped his giant whale tail. He whistled through his blowhole. "I can't think of anything I'd like better!"

Answer Key

page 36
1. watch
2. brush
3. photograph
4. lunch
5. north
6. leash
7. match
8. teeth

1. ch, Answers will vary
2. sh, Answers will vary
3. th, Answers will vary

page 37
th; ph; sh
ch; sh; th
th; ph; ch

page 38
duck; swing; laugh
wing; truck; sock

1. ng
2. gh
3. ck; ck
4. ng; gh
5. ng; ng; ng
6. ng; ng
7. ck; ck; ng

page 39
gh; ng; ng; ng; ng; ng; ck;
gh; ck; ck; ng; ck; ng; ng;
ng

ck
luck
track
clock
block

gh
tough
enough

ng
swimming
running
biking
long
training
belong
everything
finishing
anything

page 40
knot; wrinkle; knight

1. never
2. wrinkle
3. scissors
4. knob
5. seven
6. wrapper
7. nest
8. rail

page 41
1. writer
2. Knead
3. wrestling
4. scent
5. knows
6. scientist
7. knit
8. wreaths

1. wrong
2. scent
3. knight
4. scissors
5. wrap

page 42
hatchet; sleigh; pitcher
flashlight; stretch; thumb
hopscotch; lamb; night

comb; crutch; stoplight

page 43

1. thumb come			6. comb dome		
2. sleigh way			7. climb dime		
3. limb slim			8. straight hate		
4. flight fright			9. stitch rich		
5. scratch batch			10. lamb Sam		

1. sketch
2. crumbs
3. sight
4. itches
5. might
6. sunlight
7. limb

page 44
1. thunder
2. thirteen
3. sandwich
4. sheep
5. king
6. black
7. laugh
8. phone

page 45
wr; sc; ng; sh; ck
ng; ph; gh; kn, wr, th
gh, ng, gh
ng, Wh

page 46
trash; tank; clam
fan; cab; math

1. Cass, and, Matt, tanks
2. plan, and, cash
3. Grant, Cass, and, Matt, bank, and
4. man, at, hand, and, Grants, catch
5. asked, batch, plants, and
6. back, at, Cass, and, Matt

Answer Key

7. Dan, Sam, and, Max, Grants, cats

page 47
bed; neck; shell
tent; dress; sled

page 48
sick; bib; ship
cliff; grill; twins

1. Big
2. ringing
3. hitched
4. films
5. lit
6. still
7. wind

page 49
mop; knock; ox
frog; lock; pond

1. sock
2. hop
3. rock
4. top
5. blond

page 50
jump, fluff; sun, lunch; rug, junk; thumb, scrub; truck, mud; skunk, dust

1. drums
2. strums, hums

3. thumps, drummer's
4. puffs, trumpet
5. clutches, trusty
6. chugs, cup, punch
7. shuts, plugs

page 51
short a	short e	short i
has	them	kids
than	gets	things
that	tells	Civil
ask	check	ship
		visits
		trip

short o	short u
dogs	ducks
lots	up
got	mummy

page 52
1. cap + e = cape
2. sam + e = same
3. man + e = mane
4. past + e = paste
5. hat + e = hate
6. mad + e = made
7. pal + e = pale
8. rag + e = rage

sale
plane
cage
tape
came
fade
taste
rate

1. wage
2. quake
3. vane
4. vase
5. cave
6. waste

page 53
1. mice, spice, white, rice.
2. dive, tide, spines, spikes, stripes
3. dine, nice, slice, lime, ripe, vine
4. wise, hike, nine, miles, rise
5. swine, glide, slide, slime, time, fine
6. Wipe, shine, side, pile,

twice
7. five, fine, kites, twine
8. bride, glide, five, miles, while, skydives

1–4. Answers will vary but should include long **i** words with the **i-consonant-e** spelling.

page 54
nose; rope; smoke
toe; globe; bone

1. doe
2. mole
3. Rome
4. joke
5. home
6. rose
7. whole

page 55
1. cube
2. rude
3. plume
4. tune
5. dude
6. cute
7. fuse

1. June; Sue
2. rule; due
3. tune; flute
4. cute; mule
5. clues

page 56
plate, Answers will vary.;
nine, Answers will vary.;
cone, Answers will vary.
glue, Answers will vary.;
dice, Answers will vary.;

Answer Key

cake, Answers will vary.
bike, Answers will vary.;
rose, Answers will vary.;
whale, Answers will vary.

page 57

long a
state
make
name
Lake

long i
shines
Pine
Line

long o
home
close
Lone
vote

long u
clue
blue

page 58
1. short
2. long
3. long
4. long
5. short
6. short
7. short
8. long
9. short
10. long
11. short
12. short

1. hot pot; short **o**
2. mad dad; short **a**
3. space place; long **a**
4. best nest; short **e**
5. cute flute; long **u**
6. twin grin; short **i**
7. whale sale; long **a**

page 59
long **i**; short **u**; long **o**;
short **u**; short **i**; shirt **e**;
short **a**; long **i**; short **a**;
long **i**; short **e**; short **u**;
short **a**; long **a**; short **i**;
long **i**; short **a**; long **a**

page 60
1. bait
2. neigh
3. day
4. Maine
5. veil
6. jay
7. snail
8. eight

page 61
trail; Rail; train; mail; freight;
remained; paid; laid;
Maine; straight; may; away;
day; reins

page 62
beak; bee; movie
wheel; thief; peach

tree	pea	shield
seed	treat	field
three	reach	collie
sneeze	sea	piece
creek	beat	niece
speech	plead	chief

page 63
1. ee
2. ea
3. ie
4. ea
5. ee
6. ee
7. ee
8. ie
9. ea
10. ea
11. ea
12. ea; ea
13. ee

page 64
1. tight
2. thigh
3. wild
4. midnight
5. blind
6. kind
7. child
8. behind
9. flashlight
10. mind

page 65
1. child
2. right
3. wind
4. light
5. find
6. high
7. midnight
8. wild

1. sing
2. whip
3. sling
4. trip
5. flip
6. chin
7. bit
8. hint

Answer Key

page 66
cold; toast; snow

1. road
2. Coach
3. gold
4. most
5. known
6. goal

page 67

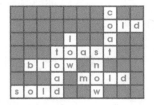

1. most
2. foam
3. row
4. scold
5. coast
6. mow

page 68
beach; peach
goat; float
thigh; sigh
hay; tray
knee; three
cold; bold
tail; rail
snow; glow
eight; weight

1. sail
2. bay
3. rip
4. flap

page 69
long **e** as in *pea*: sea; weak;
leaves; teach

long **e** as in *beep*: seen;
deep; keeps; feels; need
long **e** as in *chief*: piece;
fields
long **i** as in *night*: knight;
upright
long **i** as in *child*: wild
long **a** as in *day*: sway; stay

page 70
moose; Answers will vary.
screw; Answers will vary.
hook; Answers will vary.

good; books; few;
cartoons; Pooh; kangaroo;
gloomy; crew; grew;
school; too; knew

page 71
1. chew   stew
2. zoo   drool
3. spoon   flew
4. stood   brook
5. hoot   dew
6. gloom   loop
7. foot   hood
8. goose   snooze

moon; moon; looks; moons;
moon; loom; moon; took;
good; knew; moon; moons;
too; moons; new; moon;
Moon; Moon; Moon; Moon;
Moon;

page 72
1. bawl
2. law
3. caught
4. dawn
5. slaw
6. launch

7. gnaw
8. raw

1. crawl
2. lawn
3. author
4. yawn
5. August
6. paw
7. auto
8. saw
9. fawn
10. straw

page 73
aw   au   aw
aw   aw   au

1. launch
2. author
3. taught
4. because
5. jigsaw
6. sausage

page 74
1. oy
2. oy
3. oy
4. oy
5. oi
6. oi

1. Roy, Troy, McCoy,
   cowboys
2. annoy, loyal
3. Roy, joined, voyage
4. Troy, enjoys, coiled
5. Troy, Roy, pointing, noise
6. McCoy, broiled
7. boiled, sirloin, foil,
   cowboys

Answer Key

page 75

1. oil — royal, enjoy, ballpoint
2. coin — noise, broiler, join
3. loyal — joy, spoil, avoid
4. soy — soil, choice, boy
5. joint — point, moist, foil
6. choice — poison, voice, tinfoil

1. soy
2. coins
3. loyal
4. voice
5. noise
6. spoil
7. point
8. joined

page 76
cloud, proud; clown, brown; house, blouse

1. Brown
2. proud
3. cloud
4. hound
5. doghouse
6. ground

page 77
1. grouch
2. howl
3. flour
4. frown
5. pound
6. sour
7. plow

1. trout
2. scowl
3. pouch
4. gown
5. hour
6. town
7. growl

page 78

1. a cozy place for reading — book nook
2. a dog that eats too much — round hound
3. a fun place to swim — cool pool
4. a group of people who make soup — stew crew
5. the nose of a fish — trout snout
6. a trusty queen — loyal royal
7. a home for a rodent — mouse house
8. a bird that got away — loose goose

1. straw
2. coins
3. pounce
4. flew
5. stood

page 79

spoon	saw	cow
flew	lawn	bounce
boot	caught	gown
brew	sauce	prowl
zoo	draw	hour

hawk, found, caught, join, good, food, enjoy, schools, owl, without

page 80
1. long **e**
2. long **i**
3. long **e**
4. **y**
5. long **i**
6. long **e**
7. **y**

1. forty
2. dry
3. jelly
4. young
5. penny
6. yellow

page 81

long **i**	long **e**	**y**
Tyler	only	yo-yo
try	party	years

fly
city
tricky
easy
country
exactly
lately
baby

shiny
city
tricky
easy

yank
yet
young

page 82
1. e

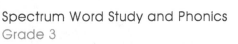

2. i
3. a
4. f
5. b
6. j
7. c
8. d
9. g
10. h

page 83
1. er
2. ir; er
3. er; er
4. ur
5. ur; er
6. ur
7. ir; ir
8. er; er

1. **herd**, shirt
2. **perk**, under
3. **purse**, girl
4. **birthday**, fern
5. **curve**, chirp
6. **dirty**, person

page 84

Answer Key

corn   **shark**
thorn   arch
sport   cart
porch   scar
cord   tart

1. large
2. garden
3. fork
4. yarn
5. snore
6. north

page 85
farmers'; morning; farms;
markets; stores; far;
charged; for; large; corn;
more; pork; Organic; arts;
garden; cart; start; larger

page 86
1. scarf
2. spy
3. after
4. horse
5. family
6. yam
7. jar
8. letter
9. yolk
10. turtle

page 87

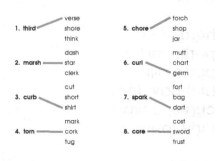

1. third — verse / shore / think
2. marsh — dash / star / clerk
3. curb — cut / short / shirt
4. torn — mark / cork / tug
5. chore — torch / shop / jar
6. curl — mutt / chart / germ
7. spark — fort / bag / dart
8. core — cost / sword / trust

1. dry, fry, my, long **i**
2. baby, bunny, lucky,
   pretty, long **e**
3. Yesterday, Yoko, yelled,
   yellow, **y**
4. fly, sky, long **i**

page 88

Base Word	Add ed	Add ing
chop	chopped	chopping
hike	hiked	hiking
bloom	bloomed	blooming
plan	planned	planning
spy	spied	spying
hope	hoped	hoping
hum	hummed	humming
carry	carried	carrying
suggest	suggested	suggesting
clap	clapped	clapping
try	tried	trying
act	acted	acting
hug	hugged	hugging

page 89
located; moving;
interviewed; allowed;
examined; passed;
traveling; cried; starting;
seeing; stopped

1. study
2. quiz
3. live
4. marry

page 90
1. barks
2. coaxes
3. studies
4. rings
5. latches
6. kisses
7. empties
8. waxes

page 91
1. tosses
2. rushes
3. tries, crashes

4. calls, watches
5. wags, brings
6. kisses, gives
7. hurries, buries

1. mix
2. fry
3. talk
4. crunch
5. marry
6. brush
7. clap
8. cry
9. hiss
10. dance
11. wash
12. bake

page 92
1. hottest
2. driest
3. wettest
4. wetter
5. sunnier
6. coldest

page 93

Base Word	Add er	Add est
safe	safer	safest
thin	thinner	thinnest
sweet	sweeter	sweetest
warm	warmer	warmest
strange	stranger	strangest
busy	busier	busiest

1. friendliest
2. quieter
3. largest
4. gentler
5. fluffiest
6. thinner
7. smarter

l blend: Blossom; Blaze;
fluffiest

Answer Key

r blend: Brady; friendliest; friendlier; Bridget; brothers; bright

page 94

Base Word	Add s or es	Add ed	Add ing
watch	watches	watched	watching
taste	tastes	tasted	tasting
finish	finishes	finished	finishing
skip	skips	skipped	skipping
miss	misses	missed	missing
relax	relaxes	relaxed	relaxing
laugh	laughs	laughed	laughing
try	tries	tried	trying
jump	jumps	jumped	jumping
explore	explores	explored	exploring
fuss	fusses	fussed	fussing
drip	drips	dripped	dripping
worry	worries	worried	worrying

page 95

1. smaller
   Answers will vary.
2. strangest
   Answers will vary.
3. funniest
   Answers will vary.
4. biggest
   Answers will vary.

liked; bigger; working; gentlest; braver; quitting; talking; making; founded; pleased; touches

page 96

cherry; cherries
dress; dresses
wheel; wheels
ball; balls
baby; babies
knife; knives

1. families
2. coaches
3. teammates
4. bases

page 97

1. party
2. thief
3. spoon
4. pony
5. peach
6. dolphin
7. class
8. diary
9. leaf

t	h	i	e	v	e	s	j	x	s
h	e	p	e	a	c	h	e	s	a
n	d	o	l	p	h	i	n	s	u
r	i	n	e	t	h	x	c	q	a
c	a	l	g	a	t	o	l	r	k
b	r	e	u	d	n	y	a	a	s
o	l	s	p	o	o	n	s	t	t
f	e	k	t	f	p	j	s	o	b
y	s	r	l	e	a	v	e	s	v
w	p	a	r	t	i	e	s	d	l

page 98

1. children
2. sheep
3. women
4. moose
5. geese

1. sheep
2. geese
3. mouse; mice
4. men

page 99

1. moose; S
2. trout; P
3. children; P
4. feet; P
5. series; S
6. die; S
   dice; P

1. b
2. a
3. a

4. b

page 100

1. Will's homework
2. the squirrel's tale
3. the computer's keyboard
4. the school's gym
5. Charles's eyes
6. the movie's actors
7. the library's books
8. Malika's smile
9. the dress's colors

1. PL
2. PO
3. PL
4. PO
5. PO

page 101

1. the campers' tents
2. the boys' sleeping bags
3. the campfires' flames
4. the crickets' chirping
5. the children's singing
6. the backpacks' zippers
7. the flashlights' beams
8. the food's smells

chirping   children   flashlights
crickets   backpacks

page 102

1. SP
2. PP
3. PL
4. SP
5. PP
6. PP
7. PL
8. SP

Answer Key

1. a
2. b
3. a
4. a

canary, cats', cage
guinea
gerbils

page 103
1. The sisters' teacher is Mrs. Huong.
2. The bus's schedule is posted on the bulletin board.
3. The lyrics are on the inside of the CD's case.
4. Antoine's friend will be here at noon.
5. The game's pieces are still inside the box.
6. The butterflies' wings seem to shimmer in the sunlight.
7. Be careful not to let go of the balloons' strings.
8. The painting's frame is cracked.
9. The skaters' jackets were warm and cozy.
10. The alarm clock's ring is loud and shrill.

page 104

Singular	Plural	Singular Possessive	Plural Possessive
book	books	book's	books'
woman	women	woman's	women's
wolf	wolves	wolf's	wolves'
egg	eggs	egg's	eggs'
library	libraries	library's	libraries'
sheep	sheep	sheep's	sheep's
mouse	mice	mouse's	mice's
dish	dishes	dish's	dishes'
city	cities	city's	cities'

1. schools; Answers will vary.
2. buses; Answers will vary.
3. leaves; Answers will vary.
4. beaches; Answers will vary.
5. countries; Answers will vary.
6. computers; Answers will vary.
7. stories; Answers will vary.
8. foxes; Answers will vary.

page 105
PL; SP; PL; PP; PL, SP

1. Muir's
2. grizzlies
3. tribes
4. trees'
5. species
6. Grasses
7. Hikers
8. families
9. deer
10. wolves
11. rangers'

page 106
1. fingernail
2. popcorn
3. starfish
4. doorbell
5. football
6. horseback
7. sunflower
8. wheelchair

1. note, book
2. back, yard
3. sand, box
4. snow, ball
5. tea, spoon
6. news, paper

page 107

1. ear	food
2. lawn	mill
3. light	work
4. sea	mower
5. scare	crow
6. home	ring
7. wind	set
8. sun	house

earring
lawnmower
lighthouse
seafood
scarecrow
homework
windmill
sunset

1. lunchroom
2. pinecone
3. nightgown
4. washcloth
5. newspaper
6. sailboat
7. spaceship

page 108

1. he would	I'll
2. I will	she's
3. did not	you've
4. have not	haven't
5. she is	he'd
6. they are	weren't
7. were not	didn't
8. you have	they're

1. hasn't
2. She's
3. wasn't
4. He'll
5. shouldn't
6. That's

page 109
1. are
2. will
3. I'm
4. would/had
5. she's
6. is/has
7. could
8. I've
9. are
10. he

1. don't; do not
2. doesn't; does not
3. they'd; they would

Answer Key

4. can't; can not
5. What's; What is

page 110
1. I'm
2. He'll
3. haven't
4. they're
5. We've
6. It's
7. won't

1. Who is; Who's
2. We will; We'll
3. can not; can't
4. has not; hasn't
5. She has; She's
6. would not; wouldn't

page 111
1. they have; **ha**
2. what is; **i**
3. we are; **a**
4. did not; **o**
5. let us; **u**
6. that is; **i**
7. I am; **a**
8. should not; **o**
9. she will; **wi**
10. would have; **ha**

1. shouldn't
2. We're
3. I've
4. won't
5. Don't
6. could've

th; wh; sh

page 112
cupcake; bedroom;
motorcycle; anteater;

rainbow;
backpack;waterfall;
teacup; airplane

1. backseat; backyard;
   backbone
2. birdbath; birdcage;
   birdseed
3. fireworks; firefly;
   fireplace; firestorm
4. sunshine; sunburn;
   sunrise; sunbath
5. snowflake; snowstorm
6. toothbrush; toothpaste

page 113

page 114
1. unable; not able
2. disagree; not agree
3. dislike; not like
4. unsure; not sure
5. unequal; not equal
6. distrust; not trust

1. unpack; Answers will
   vary.
2. disappear; Answers will
   vary.
3. unplug; Answers will vary.
4. disobey; Answers will
   vary.

page 115

1. impolite — not patient
2. incorrect — not complete
3. invisible — not correct
4. impatient — not possible
5. inexpensive — not polite
6. impossible — not exact
7. incomplete — not expensive
8. inexact — not visible

1. indirect
2. impolite
3. impure
4. incorrect
5. indoors
6. impossible

page 116
1. preorder
2. repack
3. misread
4. prewash
5. recheck
6. premix
7. misjudge

1. recount; to count again
2. predawn; before dawn
3. misconnect; connect
   badly
4. precook; cook before
5. resell; to sell again
6. misname; to name
   wrongly

page 117
1. overcharge
2. underweight
3. underdress
4. overcook
5. underrate
6. oversize

1. underwater
2. overrated
3. underline
4. overthink

Answer Key

5. overslept
6. underground

page 118
1. messy; Answers will vary.
2. quickly; Answers will vary.
3. bouncy; Answers will vary.
4. softly; Answers will vary.
5. easily; Answers will vary.
6. lucky; Answers will vary.

1. strongly
2. rusty
3. safely
4. tricky
5. steamy
6. noisily

page 119
1. teacher
2. painter
3. sailor
4. inventor
5. farmer
6. governor

1. a person who sculpts
2. a person who collects
3. a person who gardens
4. a person who builds
5. a person who runs

page 120

page 121
1. bendable
2. breakable
3. hidden
4. strengthen
5. broken

1. harden; to make hard
2. lovable; able to be loved
3. washable; able to be washed
4. widen; to make wider
5. sharpen; to make sharp

page 122
1. e
2. a
3. b
4. f
5. c
6. d

1. unafraid
2. rethought
3. prearranged
4. overload
5. unsure
6. mislead

page 123
1. actor; Answers will vary.
2. stormy; Answers will vary.
3. beautiful; Answers will vary.
4. valuable; Answers will vary.

1. sleepily
2. endless
3. darken
4. fixable
5. leader

page 124
balloon, 2; tree, 1; kangaroo, 3
pretzel, 2; bicycle, 3; monkey, 2

1. Which two picture names have the vowel sound you hear in *goose*?
   balloon   kangaroo
2. Which two picture names begin with a two-letter blend?
   Circle the blend.
   (tr)ee   (pr)etzel

page 125
1. air/plane
2. dis/like
3. pic/ture
4. cook/book
5. re/fill
6. bath/tub
7. bee/hive
8. pre/heat
9. lum/ber
10. un/do

1. Mon/day, den/tist, tooth/ache
2. win/ter, foot/prints, side/walk
3. sun/light, in/doors
4. Wel/come, some/one
5. un/tied, hall/way
6. dis/like, of/fice

page 126
1 syllable	2 syllables
wind	sea/shore
bench	un/lock
shrimp	ta/ble
fish	lad/der
star	si/lent
breeze	home/sick

3 syllables
cu/cum/ber
won/der/ful

pop/u/lar
ter/ri/ble
ad/ven/ture
el/e/phant

1. mitten
2. vacation
3. sled
4. before
5. factory
6. pinch
7. paper
8. hammer
9. loose

page 127
1. Hurricane, Katrina
2. Many, people, around, wanted
3. Maryland, difference
4. started, Project, Backpack
5. Jackie, Jenna, Kantor, backpacks, along
6. They, reached, their, goal, of
7. around, country, about, project
8. They, in, their, own, too
9. areas, Katrina
10. Even, Kantor, sisters, only, thousands, never, even

1. many
2. Coast
3. goal

page 128
wink, 1; mailbox, 2;
banana, 3; mosquito, 3;
snowflake, 2; pear, 1

2; 2
1; 1
2; 2
2; 2
3; 3
2; 2
3; 3
1; 1
2; 2
2; 2

page 129
1. puzzle; insect
2. snake; rug
3. pumpkin; notebook
4. fish; bowl
5. butterfly; forever

cac/tus; most/ly; ar/e/as;
con/di/tions; Un/like;
In/stead; pro/tect; des/ert;
an/i/mals; wa/ter; flesh/y;
in/to; o/ther; o/ver; wi/der
a/bout; spe/cies;
South/west; Mex/i/co

page 130
pail; smile; present
rabbit; hat; rip

1. terrific
2. sleepy
3. giant
4. destroy
5. giggle

page 131

1. end   beautiful
2. easy   mend
3. shut   near
4. pretty   finish
5. throw   simple
6. glad   close
7. jump   hop
8. close   toss
9. fix   happy

1. pick
2. tug
3. quiet
4. stop
5. broke
6. scream
7. small
8. see
9. keep

page 132
1. bottom
2. white
3. friend
4. morning
5. down
6. hate
7. under

n	m	r	u	n	d	e	r	v	a
q	d	b	b	j	a	r	h	p	l
b	o	t	t	o	m	c	a	z	x
o	w	p	l	y	o	e	t	g	l
n	u	n	f	r	i	e	n	d	
s	d	r	t	n	n	q	o	a	p
d	g	m	w	h	i	t	e	w	n
r	z	t	t	w	n	o	u	n	h
e	g	c	f	e	g	r	h	n	e

1. white
2. friend

page 133
short; bad; easy; smaller;
weaker; slower; woman;
less; finished; lost; fake;
boring

page 134
1. A
2. S
3. S
4. A
5. S
6. A

Answer Key

7. A
8. S
9. S
10. A
11. S
12. A

1. messy
2. full
3. lost
4. ill
5. wrong
6. infant
7. west
8. noisy
9. find
10. smooth

page 135
1. largest
2. country
3. new
4. makes
5. easier
6. grows
7. autumn
8. first
9. long
10. lost

page 136
bear; shoe; eye
eight; pear; sun
night; flower; ant

eight   night   knight

page 137
1. Answers will vary but should include the correct use of *cent*.
2. Answers will vary but should include the correct use of *close*.

3. Answers will vary but should include the correct use of *meat*.
4. Answers will vary but should include the correct use of *hear*.

1. bye; buy
2. four; for
3. high; hi
4. road; rode
5. they're; there

page 138
1. Answers will vary. Possible answer: A fly is sitting on the picnic table.
2. Answers will vary. Possible answer: Casey is up to bat next.
3. Answers will vary. Possible answer: Daisy has a loud bark.
4. Answers will vary. Possible answer: What is today's date?
5. Answers will vary. Possible answer: The bikes are in the yard.
6. Answers will vary. Possible answer: Strawberry jam is my favorite.
7. Answers will vary. Possible answer: That pen leaked ink on my shirt!
8. Answers will vary. Possible answer: Tell me a story, Mom.

page 139
1. b
2. a
3. a
4. b

5. a
6. b
7. b
8. a

1. Which two words have the long I sound?
   fine   kind

2. Which two words have a silent consonant? Circle the consonant.
   pitcher   watch

page 140
1. S
2. M
3. M
4. M
5. S
6. S
7. M
8. S

1. Answers will vary. Possible answer: a cat's.
2. Answers will vary. Possible answer: a hundred bees.
3. Answers will vary. Possible answer: honey.
4. Answers will vary. Possible answer: marbles.

page 141
Fiona and Nora walked down the sandy path to the beach. It was the middle of the day, and the sand felt like hot coals under their bare feet. They walked faster, trying not to let their feet touch the sand for long. The water was a blue carpet stretching out toward the sky. It looked cool and inviting from the hot beach.

"It's beautiful here, isn't it?" said Nora. She turned her face to the sun that hung like a fat, yellow grapefruit in the sky. Nora sniffed the salty breeze. "The ocean air smells as fresh as clean laundry."

The girls found their parents and spread out their towels. They were careful not to wake their dad, who slept like a baby under a large umbrella. Suddenly, Fiona spotted a pelican. It was a missile zooming toward the water. A moment later, it flew away with a wriggling fish sticking out of its beak. "There's always something going on at the beach!" laughed Fiona.

1. house; dinosaur
2. stomachs; bottomless pits
3. Marcus's legs; rubber

Answer Key

page 142

hair; horse; bee
deer; ring; muscle

1. sale
2. Meet, hour
3. peak
4. Your

Answers will vary. Possible answers shown.
1. Dad chopped some wood for the fire.
   Would you like to go to my softball game?
2. There is only one apple left.
   Quinn won the first game of checkers.
3. I like my pizza plain.
   The plane landed two hours late.

page 143

1. A tear rolled down the girl's cheek.
2. The seal has thick, gray fur.
3. Rest quietly until lunch.
4. We never use the old well in the yard.
5. What's inside the box?

1. S; rain, tiny footsteps
2. M; Britta, apple of my eye
3. M; snow, a thick, white blanket
4. S; heavy meal, a rock
5. S; children, mice

tiny; proudly; heavy

page 144

1. 2, 3, 1
2. 2, 1, 3
3. 1, 3, 2
4. 1, 3, 2
5. 3, 2, 1
6. 2, 3, 1

1. hers, line, mile, minnow
2. skunk, sled, sleigh, sloth
3. net, news, nibble, niece

1. phase
2. sloth, sleigh, sled

page 145

Bloomers!
Coming on Home Soon
High as a Hawk
The House of Wisdom
Piggins
Squids Will Be Squids
Superfudge

page 146

1. fork
2. dice
3. pink
4. herself
5. wing

1–5. Answers will vary.

forgave, format, forty, fork, hickory

page 147

ball * bandage
ballet
balloon
bamboo
band
balmy

bark * bath
base
barrel
barn
batch
basket

bit * blaze
blame
black
blade
blanket
blast

1. 220
2. 84
3. 85
4. 222
5. 85
6. 220
7. 84
8. 222
9. 85
10. 222
11. 220
12. 85
13. 84
14. 222
15. 220
16. 84
17. 85
18. 222

page 148

1. lesson
2. hide
3. activity
4. wrap
5. scold
6. hungry
7. fox
8. trip
9. carry
10. laugh
11. thin
12. wash

1. 2
2. no
3. 2

Answer Key

page 149
enjoy; record; book; adult;
publish; children; call;
folktale; write; write; kid;
story; tale; tiger; spot

born; recorded

page 150
Babbitt, Natalie
Banks, Lynne Reid
Byars, Betsy
Christopher, Matt
Cleary, Beverly
Dahl, Roald
Lasky, Kathryn
Lowry, Lois
Pinkney, Jerry
Wallace, Bill
White, E. B.

1. glasses; glad • globe
2. flower; floppy • flute
3. spoon; sponge • sprout

page 151
1. spaniel, sparkle, story
2. stories
3. sparkle
4. story
5. sparkle
6. 1

1. rag, rain, recycle, reflect
2. beach, cry, fling, slide
3. fan, fast, father, feast
4. invite, island, ladybug,
   lamp